D1485034

GONF

GONE TO STUD

Jane Glenn

J.A. Allen
London

British Library Cataloguing in Publication Data
A catalogue record for this book is available
from the British Library

ISBN 0.85131.658.1

Published in Great Britain in 1996 by
J.A. Allen and Company Limited,
1 Lower Grosvenor Place,
Buckingham Palace Road,
London, SW1W 0EL.

Design by Nancy Lawrence
Cartoons by Dan Lish
Typeset in Gt. Britain by Textype Typesetters
Printed in Hong Kong

CONTENTS

———•———

LIST OF CARTOONS

—◆—

INTRODUCTION

———•———

T HE FRENZY OF ACTIVITY that is packed into the five-month breeding season on a Thoroughbred stud farm is mind-boggling. Little is left to nature in an industry where hundreds of thousands of pounds can rest on a successful coupling. While lovestruck men and women await St. Valentine's Day with keen anticipation, the human and equine residents of stud farms throughout the country will be flexing their muscles in readiness for the official start to the stud season on the 15th February.

Stallions are subjected to explicit veterinary attention before they are allowed even a sniff of a mate, while mares suffer the indignities of manual examinations, stitches and swabs, not to mention the ritual of 'teasing'. Both stallions and mares must be rigorously tested for sexually transmitted diseases and have their fertility potential studied under a microscope. Though incest is out, in-breeding is common. Pedigree experts will pour over four generations in an effort to find the perfect match; there is even a computer programme available: 'Computer Mating'.

The majority of the workforce on a stud farm is made up of 'stud hands'. These come in all shapes and sizes, and both sexes. Promotion can carry such titles as 'second man' or 'stallion man' – in this predominantly male domain, few concessions are given to the female of the human species.

Horse breeding has a language of its own. A mare will either 'visit' a stallion, or be 'covered' by him or 'served' by him. The official certificate confirming the mating gives first and last 'service' dates – this has nothing to do with the number of miles a mare has completed! A German stud farmer once relayed the

message that a mare had been 'seen' by the stallion. The fact that she was in foal as a result came as a pleasant surprise!

And then there are the owners. Royalty, lords, ladies and gentlemen, film stars, pop stars and politicians. There are also Smiths, Joneses and increasingly, multi-ownerships – you, too, can own a third of a leg of a horse! Some owners are more experienced breeders than others. One can usually gauge the extent of an owner's knowledge by their reaction to being told that their mare has beta haemolytic streptococci on her swab.

Whether you are an avid racing fan or simply fancy a bet on the Derby, the horse carrying your hopes – and your money – will have begun life on a stud farm. This book is about the upper echelons of stud farming, where some of the fastest horses in the world are conceived.

CHAPTER ONE

STALLIONS AND THEIR MEN

———•———

'SO MANY WOMEN, so little time' could well be the motto of a much-sought-after Thoroughbred stallion. In one five-month season, a single stallion will attempt to impregnate anything from 20 to 320 mares. The English reserve comes into play here; Ireland is the country in which the higher ratio of mares to stallion prevails.

When a male racehorse achieves notable success on the racecourse, he enhances his potential as a stallion, which in turn makes him an internationally desirable commodity. The Japanese spend millions of yen acquiring some of the best racehorses and bloodlines, while many European countries shop for their Thoroughbred seedcorn in England. There is a healthy trade between England and the USA and between England and Australasia.

Depending upon the individual horse's achievements, pedigree and conformation, his price tag as a potential stallion will range from around £200,000 to several million pounds. Such values are reserved for flat-race horses, bred fundamentally for speed. Racehorses who run over obstacles cannot do so until they are at least three years old, and they compete for much lower prize money than their counterparts on the flat, who can establish their credentials and earn huge amounts of prize money by the end of their third year.

Buying and selling these flat-race success stories is horse dealing at its very best. Offers whiz around the world by fax, frantic telephone calls are exchanged, private jets ferry key players to view horses or sign documents. Bidders guard their intentions jealously for fear of being gazumped; the best prospects will be sought by a hard core of potential purchasers.

In order to increase spending power, the practice of 'dual hemisphere covering' is becoming more common. The northern hemisphere breeding season runs from February to July; the southern hemisphere season from August to January. If, for example, an Australian and an English buyer combine forces, they can share the burden of the initial outlay and each enjoy income from stud fees in their respective seasons – a double-barrelled return on the investment.

Nowadays, moving stallions around the world is straight-forward. However, not every stallion has the temperament or, indeed, the stamina to cope with a year-round 'workload'. He will be subjected to increased risk from the travelling, stress (yes, horses suffer from stress too) and the chance of contracting a debilitating disease. There are some nasty sexually transmitted diseases among the equine population and, although strict screening procedures exist, the more mares a single stallion covers, the greater the risk.

The stud fee for a stallion will be determined to a great extent by his market value. A stallion bought for £200,000 will command a fee of around £2,500 whereas a multi-million pound purchase may stand at stud for around £100,000 or be advertised as 'fee on application'. An owner wishing to send a mare to a stallion will purchase a 'nomination', which gives them the right to send a mare to that stallion in a particular season. If a stallion is syndicated, a mare owner may purchase a share in the stallion, ownership of which includes the right to send a mare to that stallion in each stud season. (A stallion may be owned by a partnership, but few are owned outright by single individuals.)

Nominations are sold under certain terms, the most common being '1st October terms'. This means that the fee is payable on the 1st October following the stud season, provided that the mare is in foal at that stage. Mare owners will have their mares tested for pregnancy in late September; the fact that the mare was tested in foal in May or June does not guarantee that she is still in foal in September. A 'straight fee' nomination is payable on the 15th

July, the last day of the stud season, regardless of whether or not the mare is in foal. Owners purchasing under these terms will ensure that their mare is a good breeding prospect and may take out an insurance policy to cover the cost of the nomination should the mare not get in foal. A 'split fee' nomination is divided between a 'straight fee' payment and 1st October terms. For instance, if a stallion's fee is £10,000 and his nominations are sold on 'split fee' terms, there may be £5,000 to pay on the 15th July and a further £5,000 on 1st October.

If a mare is certified barren by a veterinary surgeon in September but subsequently goes on to produce a live foal (this can and does happen – even vets make mistakes) the stud fee will become payable. As every Thoroughbred foal has to be registered before being either sold at public auction or entered for a race, the stallion owner will know if a 'mistake' has been been born – so it is always best to confess straight away.

A 'live foal' fee is payable only if the mare produces a live foal the following year. A 'special live foal' fee will generally be one that is payable on 1st October terms, but is refundable if the mare does not produce a live foal. In these cases, a veterinary certificate will be required if the mare produces a stillborn foal or if the foal dies within a specified period, usually 24 or 48 hours after birth.

Yet another way to access a stallion is to enter into a 'foal sharing' contract, where the stallion owner provides the right to use the stallion and the mare owner provides the mare, with no exchange of money. The resulting offspring will then be sold at public auction and the proceeds divided between the two parties. Although this can be a successful arrangement for both parties it requires a certain amount of luck, as there is no guarantee that a saleable animal will be produced and no guarantee that a fair price will be realised at auction.

Before a stallion can commence his new career, he will need a clean bill of health from a veterinary surgeon. This will include swabs being taken from his private parts, one being a sample of pre-ejaculatory fluid – which requires some deft footwork from the vet. It is one thing to parade a mare in front of a stallion to get him excited but quite another to 'interfere' with him! Also, when a stallion first takes up stud duties, his owners have the option of taking out a 'first season infertility' insurance policy. Prospective purchasers of a stallion may also ask for a fertility test. This involves kidding the horse with a real live mare but slipping in an artificial receptacle at the optimum moment which, again, requires some quick reactions from the vet. Fertility testing is a finely tuned operation: there is the Japanese style receptacle and the Missouri style receptacle, to name but two. Each has temperature settings and can be adjusted to provide a tighter or looser fit!

Once the deal has been done, the young stallion will be transported to his new home, the 'stud'. There he will be placed in the care of one man, a 'stallion man' and kept in luxury for the duration of his career. Stallion stud farms have custom-built 'stallion units', where brass fittings on stable doors, ceramic tiles surrounding feed and water mangers and pedigree boards with gold leaf lettering are commonplace at the best establishments. Since Shergar's abduction, closed-circuit television, complete with timed recording devices, is more an essential than an optional extra.

A stallion man needs to have gained a great deal of experience in handling Thoroughbred horses. With some notable exceptions, Thoroughbred stallions are easy enough for an experienced man to handle and a mutual respect and affection will generally be established between man and beast. Indeed, the men are fiercely proud of their charges, and justifiably so. There are, however, some stallions standing at stud who are nothing short of dangerous. Out of necessity, they are kept in secure surround- ings, handling is kept to a minimum and handlers wear protective headgear. It is matter for lengthy debate whether these horses have been born bad or made bad – it is probably something of both. As a rule, these stallions do not pose a threat to mares, but only to humans which, you may say, offers a clue to the root of their evil. Thankfully, such horses are few and far between and many breeders refuse to use them, believing that their bad temperament will be passed on to their stock.

At the other end of the scale, some stallions lack the necessary virility required for the task ahead. In the case of one young stallion, no matter how delectable the mare on offer, he showed little or no interest and gazed around at everything but his

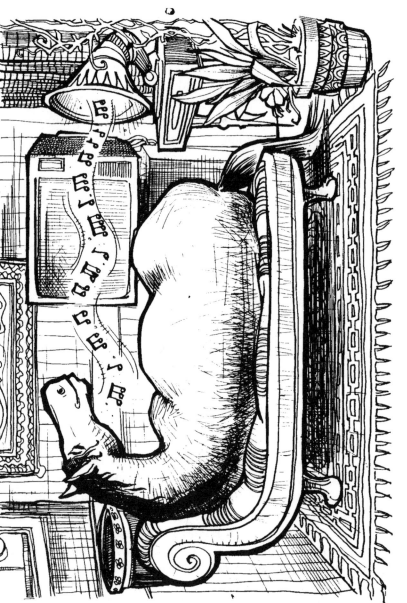

The stallion will be kept in luxury for the duration of his career

intended mate. After what seemed an eternity, he would begin to
show amorous signs and move in on the mare. Then, just as he
was about to get on with the job, a car horn would sound in the
distance or an aeroplane would be heard high above. His concentration blown, everything drooped to a halt! The enterprising
stud staff tried all sorts of aphrodisiacs: herbal remedies,
Guinness in his feed, even 'Boar Mate' – an aerosol used on
sows to encourage backward boars! The most effective aid
proved to be a particularly revolting cheap perfume sprayed onto
the mares' hindquarters – but even then he had his off-days.

Another stallion with a hit-and-miss libido showed more
interest in his man than the mares, particularly on a warm day
when the man perspired freely. The most obliging of mares
would be presented to him but until he had nuzzled his man,
licked his hand and been given soft words of encouragement, he
would show no inclination to perform. At least one of them
would appear to have job security – although the stallion man's
wife did reveal that the horse had also taken a passing fancy to a
visiting horsebox driver!

At the beginning of the stud season, a successful stallion and
his man will need to be fit. Depending on the number of mares
booked to him, the stallion will be required to perform his duty
between one and three times a day at the height of the season.
Artificial insemination is forbidden among the Thoroughbred
population, so there are no short cuts.

A few stallions are ridden to get them fit but the majority are
simply exercised in hand – an unfortunate description, given the
nature of their work. What it actually means is the horse being
led out on exercise, on and around the stud farm, for between one
and two hours a day. They will also be lunged which, to the
uninitiated, involves the horse trotting or cantering round in large
circles while his man stands in one place, controlling the horse
with a long lungeing rein. This combination of long, slow work
and short, sharp bursts of exercise will bring the horse to peak
fitness – much like any athlete.

To protect a stallion against injury, stud managers may require
the horse to be 'dressed' for his daily exercise. Knee pads may be
worn in case he stumbles, and tendon boots fitted on his forelegs
to prevent the opposite iron-clad hoof knocking a tendon. Horses

straight out of a racing yard, with clipped coats, will wear a blanket (known as a 'sheet') to keep out the worst of the weather. The stallion will, of course, be wearing a bridle, to which his man is attached by a strong leather rein.

With the advent of slimline telephones and mobile radios, stud managers can equip the stallion man with one or the other and so maintain contact wherever the horse is taken. In an emergency, the stallion man can contact the stud office and help can be dispatched in minutes. When radios are used, the stallion man should be reminded that, with the radio fixed to his belt, it is easy to press the transmit button inadvertently. Secrets shared between man and beast are not always fit for the open airways – neither are suggestions made by stallion men to nubile ladies who may pass their way on exercise!

When mating takes place, it is the mare who will require 'dressing'. If she is nervous or playing hard to get, she may kick out as the stallion approaches. Although her iron shoes will have been removed, she is still capable of inflicting a nasty blow to a limb or, worse, to a vital organ. To soften such blows, she will have a pair of thick felt 'kicking boots' which are, in effect, felt overshoes, strapped to her hind feet. Some stallions are inclined, once mounted, to hold on with their teeth. In these cases, a wide leather collar will be placed over the mare's neck and withers to save her the agony of such passionate love bites.

When the happy couple are ready, willing and able, they can get down to business. If the mare is a 'maiden' (virgin) she may be fractious through sheer fright. This is where another horse, called a 'teaser', is brought into action to 'bounce' the mare. This entails the teaser approaching the mare in a very stallion-like manner and the staff actually allowing him to mount her – but that's as far as it goes. He, poor chap, will then be pulled off and taken away, leaving the stallion to move in on a slightly less frightened young filly. (The teaser's role is explained more fully in the next chapter.)

The stud manager or a senior member of staff is required to witness every mating. On stud farms where more than one stallion is resident, this is not least to make sure that the right mare is mated with the right stallion. Such errors could potentially be the subject of costly compensation cases – hardly surprising when the value of the offspring can vary by tens of thousands of pounds depending upon parentage. The most modern studs keep a video recording of each mating – which are pretty monotonous viewing, but foolproof.

Despite the large number of female staff employed on stud farms they are rarely, if ever, employed as stallion men – or stallion persons. Indeed, stud managers still exist who refuse to have women present to witness the matings. Whether this is to save potential embarrassment to the men or an attempt to preserve an all-male domain is debatable! On the other hand, half a ton of rampant stallion in a determined state of mind would be a double handful for any woman, no matter how experienced.

Once a mare has been mated with the stallion, the next step, between 16 and 20 days later, is to scan her for pregnancy. This is when competition between stallion men hots up, particularly in the Newmarket area where the highest concentration of stallions is to be found. The number of mares scanned in foal from their first service is a matter of honour among the men. For those in charge of 'first season' stallions, this is a nail-biting time, particularly if the first few mares scanned prove not to be in foal. That this will not necessarily be a failure on the stallion's part is no consolation at this crucial time. Once the first dozen or so positive scans are out of the way, things relax a little and stallion men will revert to their usual camaraderie over a pint or three in the local pub. Provided that their 'boys' progress well through the season, peace reigns, at least until the season's end. By the 15th July, they will have a good idea how many mares each stallion has got in foal: much will be made of those men with stallions showing a fertility rate of over 90 per cent.

You might think that the title 'stallion man' would give rise to much boasting among the men. This, on the whole, is not the case; if they boast of anything it is of the horses, not themselves. But not so one young man who, relatively inexperienced, was given the opportunity to look after two stallions. He never missed a chance to use his title, boasting to the girls of his own sexual prowess. However, one of the stallions in his care was of an unpredictable nature. Instead of keeping his mind on the job, the lad strutted around, full of his own importance. The stallion was quick to see through this 'all mouth and trousers' attitude and, after some nasty moments and near misses, he frightened the lad off the job for good. One day he cornered the lad in the stable and, in all seriousness, would probably have caused him grievous bodily harm if the lad hadn't made a dive for the door. The lad demoted himself to looking after the mares whom, having learnt his lesson, he treated well and with respect. The stallion never forgot; whenever he saw the lad across the yard he would lay back his ears and bare his teeth in the most menacing way.

One of the kindest stallion men I ever came across was a quiet, gentle man who looked after his horses extremely well. He was not, however, blessed with great intelligence – a fact which often caused the stud groom to despair. A hydroponic grass machine, which would provide the means to feed the stallions succulent grass in the middle of winter, had just been acquired by the stud manager. The seed had to be soaked to speed up germination and the stallion man was told to place the grain in a plastic bucket with some holes in it, through which any excess water could drain. The stallion man shut himself in the feed shed, where the stud groom found him two hours later. He had made two large holes in the bottom of the bucket and had been trying for all that time to work out how to soak the grain without it running out of these holes.

The position of stallion man is the target for many a stud hand on his way up the ladder. The turnover among stud grooms, second men and stallion men is low, with opportunities on good stallion studs few and far between. Apart from the prestige of looking after the stallions, there are undoubtedly extra 'perks' to be had by a stallion man. Each season the stallion man will be in receipt of the lion's share of the 'groom's fees' which can amount to a tidy sum, even after tax. A 'groom's fee' is traditionally paid each season to the stallion stud by the owner of each mare who is mated with the stallion that season. These fees, generally between £30 and £50 per mare, are shared between the stallion man, the stud groom and then the rest of the stud staff at the end of the season. (This groom's fee should not be confused with the stud fee, payable for each mare visiting the stallion, which is reckoned in thousands rather than tens of pounds.)

With the stud season over, high summer is the time when, resplendent in their summer coats, stallions will be professionally photographed to produce material for advertisements in bloodstock magazines later in the year. Although the horses are looked after superbly throughout the year, the final spit and polish for the camera is an art in itself. The equine fashion pages are studied in minute detail by mare owners. 'No foot, no horse' is as true for the racehorse breeder as it was for any kingdom-seeking knight. In order to photograph the horse on emerald green grass and still show his feet, an area of the best paddock – or the stud manager's lawn – will be mown to bowling green standard. Mane and tail will be brushed and trimmed to just the right length and the gleam on a horse's coat may be enhanced by a light wiping of baby oil – particularly effective in bringing out the sheen on a grey coat.

There is a right way and a wrong way for a stallion to pose for the equine fashion pages, but try explaining that to an impatient stallion. He will be cajoled into standing just so, only to move a foot, flick his tail or shake his head at precisely the wrong moment. He will very soon become bored by this seemingly pointless exercise and will rest a leg, stretch his neck and try to pick at the grass. He will get fed up and fractious and nip at his man, who will be doing well to keep his 'cool'. In an effort to get the horse to look up and prick his ears, all manner of distractions will be provided. Whistles, whoops, heavy metal and other strange music create the most wonderful charade. Grown men will crawl around on all fours trying to look and sound like a dog – and then the sun goes in!

Leafing through the volumes of stallion advertisements, one cannot help but wonder how the names are chosen. Racehorses are generally named when they are one or two years old, so those who go on to become stallions are not always blessed with an appropriate name – and changing a name is considered bad luck. *Dancing Brave*, *Sun Prince*, *Dashing Blade* and *Wolfhound* all have the right ring about them but, while one can understand why a racehorse may be called *Nureyev*, *Fairy King*, *Shirley Heights* or *Furry Glen*, such names do not exactly conjure up a picture of manhood. Across the Atlantic you will find *Momsfurrari*, *Northern No Trump* and *I'ma Hellraiser* – the less said the better. On the other hand, *Master Willie*, *Blushing Groom* and *New Member* would seem to have been christened with stallion duties very much in mind!

A most impressive sight, and an opportunity to compare a number of stallions at close quarters, is the annual stallion parade held at the National Stud in Newmarket. This is organised by the British Bloodstock Agency and the National Stud, and there are generally around 20 stallions on show. Each is led through a large barn and walked around under spotlights against a suitable backdrop while a commentator extols their virtues as racehorses and stallions. When they have all been through the barn, they are paraded together in three or four adjacent paddocks, and can also be viewed back in the stable areas. There are similar stallion parades at Doncaster, during the bloodstock sales in January, and at Salisbury racecourse where, in the autumn, the Wessex Stallion Parade takes place.

Stallions taking up stud duties in their first season are usually well supported. Breeders will take the view that, if a horse is going to pass on his ability, they will be a step ahead of those breeders who adopt the 'wait and see' policy. Until a stallion has his first two-year-old runners, (three years after he retires to stud), his stud fee will not warrant an increase. If his first crop contains some top class racehorses, those breeders who supported the stallion in his early years will be in an enviable position. It is, however, a high risk operation; a stallion who fails to pass on his ability will quickly find himself unwanted and on the open market.

Breeding a good racehorse who becomes a success as a stallion must surely be the ultimate aim of the racehorse breeder. Watching that horse grow and develop, following him through his early days in the training yard, the thrill of watching him win his first race, the growing belief that he is destined for the top, savouring the moments of glory as he fulfils all the promise is heady stuff indeed. Then comes the satisfaction of seeing him settled in his box at the stallion unit and seeing his achievements perpetuated through his sons and daughters on the racecourse – success breeding success.

CHAPTER TWO
MARES' TALES

———•———

M ARES ARE AS INDIVIDUAL as women. They come in as many shapes, sizes and hair colours and, very definitely, as many types of personality. Some are natural mothers, some are not; some behave in the most outrageous manner – particularly when a stallion is present, others are totally submissive.

When owners decide which stallions to use for their mares, only passing consideration is given to the location of the stallion. Consequently, some mares are better travelled than some people, whether by road, sea or air. The majority of mares moving around England, Scotland and Wales do so in horseboxes. While some are no more than cattle lorries, the top end of the horsebox market is sheer luxury. The biggest horseboxes will carry up to six mares and foals, be padded throughout, have air-conditioning and open access to the groom's area which, in turn, has open access to the cab. Cooking facilities, sleeping compartments (for grooms and drivers) and radios or mobile telephones are commonplace in these equine limousines.

Mares visiting stallions in Ireland or France will be sent either by sea or air, depending on the value of the mare, whether she is carrying a foal, and the time of year. A heavily pregnant mare will have a smoother, quicker and safer journey by air than by ferry on a rough Irish Sea or English Channel. Indeed, mares can be transported many miles to a ferry destination, only for a gale to blow up which causes the captain to refuse to ship livestock. In this case there is usually nothing for it but to return the mares to their home stud and try again another day.

Some mares travel better than others. One young mare, born

and raised on a Northumbrian stud farm, refused to load into a horsebox without her companion, Willie the bullock. Willie was duly pushed and shoved into the horsebox for the long journey south to the stallion stud. Once in the company of the mares at the stud, Willie's friend settled down happily and Willie was driven home again. Two months later the horsebox arrived, complete with Willie, to accompany the mare on her long journey home. The mare eventually grew out of this dependency and, sadly, Willie was dispatched to pastures in the sky.

Considering the number of mares being moved around the country each year, accidents are, thankfully, few and far between. Whilst awaiting the arrival of an in-foal mare one afternoon, a call came from the local police to say there had been an accident just five miles short of the mare's destination. Coming too fast on a curving, downhill stretch of road, the box driver had swerved to miss an oncoming car which was over the white line and the horsebox turned over on its side across the entrance of an overhead bridge. The local veterinary surgeon was called out and, taking his life in his hands, he crawled into the horsebox where he soothed and then tranquillised the mare. He eventually managed to lead her out of a hole the fire brigade had cut in the side of the box. She shook herself, picked at some grass on the verge, walked calmly into the replacement box and walked off at the stallion stud as cool as can be. She had a few minor cuts on her head, but was otherwise unhurt. Her foal, born on time without a hitch, went on to win two races as a two-year-old.

On arrival at the stallion stud, a mare will be introduced to a group of mares of the same status. They will either be maiden (never previously mated), barren (not in foal from the previous year's mating) or in foal. They can also be classed as barren maidens (mated the previous year for the first time but not subsequently in foal), maiden foalers (due to foal for the first time) or 'rested' (not mated the previous year). Racing fans should not confuse a maiden mare as described above with a maiden racehorse: the latter is one who has never won a race, and can be either male or female.

Owners with adequate facilities may foal their mare at home, sending the mare and foal to the stallion stud between three days and three weeks later. The daily 'keep' (boarding) charge for a mare will vary from stud to stud, but an approximate guide is between £10 and £15 for a mare without a foal and between £12 and £20 for a mare and foal. The stallion stud will also charge a foaling fee of between £120 and £200, so foaling at home is cost-effective, provided there is good back-up from a veterinary surgeon.

The practice of 'walking in' mares for covering is also a cost-effective way of breeding, but must rely heavily on the expertise of the veterinary surgeon attending the mare. The idea is that, once the mare is found in season at her owner's stud farm, she is examined by a veterinary surgeon, who will advise the optimum time for mating. A day and time is then arranged for the mare to arrive at the stallion stud. The mare will be taken off the horsebox, covered by the stallion and taken straight home again.

Mares who get in foal every year from just one covering are a blessing for both their owners and the owners of the stallion. However, mares are not machines and nature has a way of calling a halt every now and then. Most owners understand this and, provided every effort is made at the stallion stud to get the mare in foal, they accept the fact that mares will not always conceive, or maintain a pregnancy. Those owners who expect their mare to conceive every single year should compare their broodmare to a human and appreciate that life just isn't like that!

Mares can easily suffer bruising at foaling, particularly if they have a difficult birth – for example if the foal is very large. A mare can have a low-grade infection which, despite treatment, persists sufficiently to prevent conception. The older a mare gets and the more foals she has, the greater the degree of wear and tear on her reproductive tracts, no matter how well she is cared for. Hormones can also play havoc: some mares become known as 'every other year' breeders through their apparent inability to conceive when they have a foal at foot.

Not all mares foal on time. The recognised gestation period for a mare is 11 months, give or take a few days. Some mares get into a regular pattern of foaling, say, a week early each year or two weeks late each year. Others will foal up to a month late for no apparent reason. It is generally accepted that to induce a mare is to induce a problem and, for the most part, mares are left to give birth in their own time.

Since all Thoroughbreds have their official birthday on the 1st January, the earlier a foal is produced, the better. A horse born in January, competing in a race for two-year-olds, will have a distinct advantage over one born in June, running in the same race. Those mares who persistently foal late or who do not get in foal until late in the season will sometimes be given a year off (rested). This allows the mare to be covered early the following season, to produce a January or February foal, thereby bringing the whole process forward again.

Every top class stallion stud will have a purpose built foaling unit. The National Stud at Newmarket has the most delightful weathervane on its foaling complex: a stork carrying a foal. The foaling unit will usually be constructed so that, in addition to the usual half doors on the front of the stable, access is also possible from the rear, through doors opening onto a central room or corridor. These doors will also have a peephole opening so that the mares can be watched without being disturbed.

Closed-circuit television is installed in the foaling boxes, with monitors in the stud groom's or manager's house. In order to maintain a picture on the CCTV monitors, it is necessary to leave some form of lighting on in the stables. Some studs use red light bulbs which produce a subdued light but still allow the CCTV to operate – the 'red light' district! In addition to CCTV, once the foaling season starts in earnest, someone will be appointed to sit up each night in the room which adjoins the main foaling boxes. If the person sitting up is fully experienced, he or she will cope with the majority of foalings, only calling for assistance if a problem arises. However, such experienced staff are not always available so, when a mare shows obvious signs of foaling, the stud groom or foaling foreman will be summoned. As the majority of mares foal between the anti-social hours of 11 p.m. and 5 a.m., the stud groom or foaling foreman can have an exhausting season on a stud farm that foals over 50 mares.

The most obvious sign that a mare is near to foaling is when she runs milk from her teats. Before she reaches this stage, her udder, known as her 'bag', will gradually fill until she has a 'full bag'. The next stage is the appearance of a sticky substance, 'wax', which is excreted from her teats, and protrudes like small candles. When a mare produces the first wax, some people describe this as 'pushing a plug'; this progresses to 'waxing up' and 'running milk'. In an attempt to ascertain whether foaling is imminent, much attention is paid to the progression of 'bags' on each foaling mare. However, not all mares go through these stages, and a first time foaler can go into labour without much of a bag at all, let alone wax showing or milk running. Even a mare who has had several foals can sometimes surprise experienced foaling staff – which underlines the importance of total vigilance, both at night and during the day.

If an in-foal mare is travelling to the stallion stud, it is recommended that she travels one month before she is due to foal. However, not all owners follow this policy. One mare was sent 200 miles in a horsebox having already waxed up, and foaled six hours after her arrival. All was well on this occasion, but it was cutting it much too fine for comfort.

A mare may run milk for several days before foaling, which provides an opportunity for her to be gently 'milked' of the colostrum – her first milk – which is rich in antibodies. If another mare fails to produce milk (a rare occurrence), or a foal is unable to suck naturally for any reason, it is a real boon to have on hand colostrum that has been collected and deep frozen. The most crucial time to raid the colostrum bank is when a mare is lost at foaling; the orphaned foal will benefit greatly from the colostrum until being weaned on to artificial milk, or until a foster mother is found and a successful adoption takes place.

Fostering an orphan foal is an extremely skilled task. If you regularly watch racing on television, you may have seen appeals broadcast for a foster mare – a great way of spreading the word. The successes which are subsequently publicised are usually those where a common type of mare, or a cute pony mare, successfully adopts an elegant Thoroughbred foal. No matter what the foster mare's breeding, if she rears the foal well she has been worth her weight in gold.

Not all mares are natural mothers. When one of the top racing mares of the 1980s was retired to stud, she was at best indifferent towards her foals and, at worst, violent. Watching her give birth one year, I noticed that she barely got warm (most mares will sweat freely at the onset of labour), but just lay down, pushed her foal out, got up and resumed eating her hay. There was not a

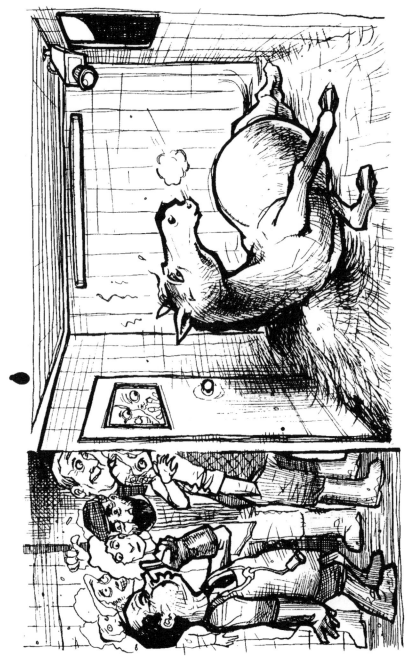

Mares can be watched without being disturbed

second glance at her foal – just an ominous twitching of the ears as the foal struggled to stand up. She did stop munching once or twice when the foal blundered into her looking for milk but, other than this, she displayed no maternal instinct at all. She adopted a look of irritation as the foal started to suck, but kept right on munching her hay. At least she was not violent towards the foal and, over the ensuing weeks, she developed sufficient maternal instinct to whinny when the foal wandered too far from her in the paddock. However, she showed little sign of distress when, later in the year, she was separated from her foal at weaning.

At the other end of the scale, an overprotective mare, described as 'foal-proud' can inadvertently hurt her foal through her very efforts to provide protection. At worst, a foal-proud mare will try to savage anyone attempting to enter the stable, let alone touch the foal. A mild tranquilliser usually does the trick – once you have caught the mare to administer it!

Mares normally come into season approximately 7–10 days after foaling and, thereafter, at intervals of between 17 and 21 days. Maiden or barren mares may be brought into season by artificial means early in the year in an attempt to get them in foal early. In advance of a course of artificial hormone to bring them into season, they may be kept 'under lights' – which is simply keeping a light on in their stable during the dark winter evenings and early in the morning, to lengthen the hours of 'daylight', and pretend spring has arrived.

Once at the stallion stud, a mare will be regularly 'teased' to find out when she is in season – this is best described as equine foreplay! Stallion studs keep a male horse, who may be a failed racehorse or a pony stallion, specifically as a 'teaser'. Some teasers are stallions in their own right and have a few mares booked to them; others never get to mate with a mare at all. Some pony teasers have had a vasectomy and can be turned out with 'shy' fillies in the paddock.

The best teaser I have ever seen in action was a part-bred Arab stallion named Micky. Micky didn't need a handler. He was put into his post-and-rail fenced yard and the mares would be led up to the fence one by one. He would stand at a respectable distance until summoned and then saunter up to the mare, ears pricked, whinnying softly. He gently sniffed and nuzzled the mare's neck through the fence, then moved on to her flanks and then her hindquarters, all the time whinnying in low, sexy tones. If you had good reason to think that a mare was in season, yet she laid her ears back and lashed out with her hind legs, you had only to say 'Harder Micky, harder!' and he would instantly become more masterful, snorting, stamping his feet and roaring in a very domineering way. Egged on to even greater heights, he would stand back a pace of two, rear up on his hind legs then plunge back towards the mare, nipping at her neck, her side and the top of her tail until even the best cheat owned up!

Before a mare can be mated with a stallion, she will need a negative clitoral swab to confirm that she is free from sexually transmitted diseases such as contagious equine metritis (CEM), klebsiella and pseudomonas. Once the mare is found in season, the vet will take a cervical swab and smear to ensure that she has no other infection that would jeopardise her chance of conception. Among the more common infections are beta haemolytic streptococci, alpha haemolytic streptococci and E. coli. Despite the sound of them, these infections are easily treated with antibiotics and uterine irrigation. One of the main concerns when a mare has a positive cervical swab result is the time factor. She will need treating during that oestrus period and will either have to wait for her next oestrus period or be 'short-cycled' before she can be covered. Short-cycling is common practice; the mare is injected with prostaglandin as an artificial means of bringing her back into season. It does not always work, but is worth trying in some cases.

Once the mare has a negative swab and smear she will be examined by the vet, who will ascertain the optimum time for mating. This is when the uninitiated come up against so much double-dutch: 'Your mare was palped this morning; she was C4 with an L 3.9 firm to soft'. Translated, this means the mare was manually examined by the vet who palpated the ovaries. On a scale of 1–4, her cervix was fully relaxed and there was a follicle on the left ovary which was firm to soft. (The follicle starts off firm, then softens before ovulation takes place – which can take anything from a few hours to several days. This is why daily examination by a vet is essential, and it is preferable if the same vet is used throughout, so that there is some continuity of monitoring.)

If you simply have the mare covered every day (or even every other day) that she is showing in season and will stand quietly for the stallion, you could end up having to cover each mare several times in each oestrus period. If a stallion has a large number of mares booked to him, it is essential to keep the number of times each mare is covered to a minimum to ensure the best chance of conception for all.

After the mare has been covered, what next? As a rule, she will be checked two days later to see whether she has ovulated. If she has, she will next be seen by the vet when she is due to be scanned for pregnancy, or if she comes back into season. If she has not ovulated, she will need covering again, a procedure referred to as 'cross-covering'. If everything, including Mother Nature, is timed correctly and there are no underlying problems, a mare should conceive with one covering – but it is not uncommon for a mare to be covered two or three times in one oestrus period before she ovulates.

By using an ultrasound scanner, veterinary surgeons can detect a pregnancy from as early as 12 days after the mare has conceived. However, as it is impossible to gauge the exact time of conception, scanning early is often inconclusive. It is therefore more usual to scan some 16 to 18 days after the mare was last covered when, if she has conceived, the foetal sac will be clearly detected. Just to confuse the issue, uterine cysts, which are not uncommon in mares, can be mistaken for a foetal sac. The sac contains fluid which shows up as a 'black hole' on the scanner picture; since a cyst is also fluid-filled, confusion is understandable.

The second scan usually takes place between 26 and 30 days after covering, when the foetal sac will have enlarged, so the early formation of the foetus can be seen and a heartbeat detected. If, at 16 days, there is what appears to be a cyst present, as well as a foetal sac, an extra scan may take place at about 20 days to determine whether the 'cyst' is actually a cyst, or whether a twin conception has taken place. The next scan, at about 40 days, will clearly show the foetus in the sac, and the vet can fill out a certificate of pregnancy with confidence.

A further manual check by the vet at around 60 days is normal practice and a final check at the end of September will determine whether or not the 1st October term stud fee is payable. It is always worth getting the vet to check a mare for pregnancy at this time of year, even if she has been pronounced not in foal in May or June. An early pregnancy can be missed by the best vet, much to the delight and amusement of the mare's owner.

Among the scientific advances in the field of equine reproduction is the ability to remove cysts by laser treatment. Mares sometimes have a cluster of cysts which may reduce the chances of conception or, if the mare does conceive, restrict the space in which the pregnancy can develop normally. Although cysts can re-form, the removal of a cluster at the right time will enable the mare to be covered again and, if she conceives, the pregnancy will have room to develop before the cysts re-form.

One of the chief uses of the ultrasound scanner is in the early detection of twins. Mares rarely carry twins safely to full term. They will usually miscarry them at some stage but, if not, complications can quickly arise. If twins do survive, they can often present problems at foaling and are never as robust as single foals. It is therefore in the best interests of the mare if one of the twin foetal sacs can be removed at an early stage.

Mares with seemingly normal, single pregnancies can still miscarry their foals for a variety of reasons. When late abortion occurs, it is always a source of concern. The Animal Health Trust's Equine Fertility Unit at Newmarket has the facilities to take in stillborn foals and test them for infectious or contagious disease, giving a preliminary report in 24 hours.

'The virus', that plagues so many racehorse trainers, can also occur on stud farms, with dire consequences. The strain of virus known as equine herpes virus 1 (EHV-1) can cause abortion and, where a group of mares live together in the same paddock, an 'abortion storm' may occur, when a whole bunch will abort their foals. This virus is highly contagious on the dead foal and membranes at the time of abortion, but can also be passed from mare to mare through nasal contact. There is now a vaccine available, Pneumabort K, which is widely used during pregnancy. It offers no guarantee but does appear to reduce the occurrence of multiple abortions in groups of mares, and abortion storms are thankfully less common than they were.

Despite all the problems that can occur on a busy stud farm, there are few sights to beat the pastoral scene of mares and foals grazing contentedly in tree-lined paddocks. Mares with foals at foot will be matched up with other mares who have foals around the same age. To watch foals taking their first steps is a wonder in itself, but to watch them making friends with other foals is the most delightful, time-wasting occupation. They are all different. The cheeky ones will be quick to stray from their mothers in search of a game while the shy ones hide behind their mothers, peeking out from behind their tails.

Some mares are slow to settle, and will trot or canter around a paddock until you feel sure the foal must be exhausted. Others simply want the quiet life, but their foals may feel differently, racing around the paddock with worried mothers anxiously in tow. As they grow up, the foals will start to play in groups. Chase-me-Charlie is all good practice for their racing days ahead – though you would have to be a more than shrewd judge to pick a winner at this stage.

The education process starts early, with a tiny foal headcollar fitted when the foal is one day old. The foals will be taught to lead so that, after a while, one person can lead a mare and foal with no assistance. The farrier will be taking a close interest in the foal's feet, as well as the mare's, from about one month old. It is at this stage that faults (such as pigeon toes) can be improved or corrected.

If you see a mare with a very short tail and a foal at foot, don't start thinking the owner has been out with the scissors. Watch for any length of time and you will see the young foal take a mouthful of mum's tail, suck at it, chew it, spit it out and start again. And that's the end of the mare's tail!

CHAPTER THREE

LABOUR OF LOVE

———•———

To the uninitiated, 'Situations Vacant' columns in publications such as *Horse and Hound* or the *Racing Post* can carry unnerving advertisements: 'Young person required for general stud duties. Salary according to age and experience', or 'Second man required for stud work. Previous experience essential. Single accommodation only'. Further confusion can arise through specialist job titles. For example, a stud farm advertising for a stud groom is not looking for an ordinary groom to work on a stud farm but a head groom, who will need a great deal of knowledge and experience.

The average stallion stud will employ a manager, a stud groom, a second man (second in command to the stud groom), a stallion man and a number of stud hands, who look after the mares and foals on the stud. There may also be a foaling foreman, responsible for overseeing all the foaling. On stud farms covering many acres, such as the National Stud at Newmarket, the stable yards are so far apart that each yard has a foreman who is responsible for the smooth running of that yard.

A stud farm is an equine version of a working country estate, with the owner, manager or stud groom in 'the big house' and the staff housed in flats or cottages on and around the stud. It is quite correct to tell H.M. Inspector of Taxes that provision of accommodation for members of staff is for the better performance of their duties. Thoroughbred horses need constant attention; being close at hand can make the difference between life and death for a mare or foal if something goes wrong in the middle of the night.

Occasionally, there will be a resident veterinary surgeon but, more usually, the stud's vet will come from a local veterinary practice that specialises in horses. The vet, or an associate, will be on call around the clock during the breeding season and will visit on a daily basis to carry out routine work.

The office staff consists of the manager and a secretary. On the very big studs there will be more than one secretary, plus a receptionist and an accountant. Stud farm work does not stop at weekends or on bank holidays and owners will expect constant access by telephone to monitor the progress of their mares. It is therefore essential to have someone manning the telephone and for staff to be available to show stallions, mares and foals to visiting owners who call in unannounced.

In addition, there will usually be at least one mainte-nance/farm man who will keep the paddocks, fencing and buildings in good order under the supervision of the stud groom. A full or part time gardener is a must. Most stallion studs have huge areas of lawns, and keeping them mown is a full time job during the summer months, while trees, hedges, flower beds, tubs and hanging baskets need attention all year round. Out of season, painting the exteriors of stables, barns and houses is essential if a public (stallion) stud is to maintain its appearance. The cleanliness of the interiors of stables (not to mention staff accommodation) is vital for the control of disease and involves much disinfecting and steam cleaning both in and out of season. There may be yearlings, mares and foals to prepare for the bloodstock sales; there is never a dull moment on a stud farm.

During the season, students are sometimes taken on for short spells. They may be second or third year veterinary students, or students from a stud management course on a work placement. It is essential that they know the basics of horse care; inexperi-enced students are a liability to the stock and to themselves. The National Stud at Newmarket runs a student training course but insists on their students having had previous experience of working on a stud farm.

To be an effective manager, it is preferable to have worked in most if not all the positions over which a manager will ultimately have control. The manager who has achieved this will not only have the respect of the employees, but will know exactly how much can be expected from them under a variety of conditions.

The manager's position is slightly less precarious than that of a football manager. Someone managing a high risk, long-term operation cannot, for instance, be entirely blamed for an infertile stallion or for failing to attract clients to use a particular stallion.

The owner-manager is a rare species today. Those who do exist generally possess a sound working knowledge of all aspects of the business, gained through years of practical experience. They may be hard taskmasters, but the majority will be held in high regard by their staff and by their clients. Never mind that the latest fads and fashions are not adopted overnight; sound horsemanship will see them through.

The younger breed of manager will have had to cover most aspects of the business in a much shorter period of time. Such people need to possess above average personnel management skills to make up for their lack of years if they are to gain the respect of stud staff who may well have started their careers in the business well before the manager was out of nappies!

As with any industry, progress is inevitable. With horses, there are the old ways, the new ways and the ways the horses like best! New ways can and do succeed, but persuading an established staff that the new way works better can be a hard climb up a very steep hill. The introduction of a new variety of feed for the mares on one stud was met with 'They won't eat it' by a stud groom of many years standing. It transpired that they wouldn't eat it, because he didn't feed it!

The younger managers will have computerisation high on the agenda. For accounting purposes this is undoubtedly an improvement on the haphazard way in which horse accounts were often kept. Cardboard boxes are all very well but, in staff hours alone, can earn a penalty from the tax inspector. From a record-keeping point of view there is a huge amount of information generated by a stallion stud, which can be stored and integrated with the right software. However, when an owner rings in for an update on their mare, they do not expect to be treated like the customer of a bank whose computer has 'gone down' that day!

The manager will need to retain a mental picture of every visiting mare and foal: the condition of each animal; the state of the mare's reproductive organs; whether the foal has crooked legs, and the exact nature of any problem that may have occurred. It is essential, therefore, that the manager is a fair judge of a horse and is sufficiently knowledgeable to offer an opinion on any aspect of mares, foals and stallions. Foals, in particular, can appear in excellent health one day and have bad diarrhoea (referred to as 'scouring') the next. Likewise, a mare may come in lame from the field or have swollen legs first thing in the morning. With good staff, the manager will keep on top of such incidents so that an owner calling in unexpectedly will not be faced with a lame mare and a scouring foal without some pre-warning.

A well-managed stallion stud will attract and maintain a loyal clientele, who will support any new stallion the stud may acquire. Owners invest a great deal in a stallion stud; not only the stud fee but the welfare costs of their mare and foal throughout their stay at the stud. A good reputation is hard won and more easily lost. Accidents will happen at the best-run stud farms, but a breeder unfortunate enough to lose a mare at stud through an unforeseeable accident does not help your cause by telling all and sundry that you 'killed the mare'.

As previously mentioned, stud groom is the title given to the head groom on a stud farm. It is the stud groom's job to liaise between manager and staff, to ensure that the methods and procedures prescribed by the manager are properly carried out, and to oversee the well-being of all the horses on the stud farm. There will also be a certain amount of paperwork to deal with: teasing lists, vet lists, covering lists, worming and farriery requirements and checking the details of mares on arrival and departure. Drawing up a list of 'time off' for staff can be a tricky business, often causing more headaches than the most difficult mare. The stud groom's responsibilities will vary, depending on the involvement of the manager. If the manager is office-orientated, the stud groom will need to monitor the progress of each stallion, mare and foal closely, reporting daily to the manager. If the manager has a good office staff, and can thus spend more time out on the stud, the stud groom can concentrate more on the 'nuts and bolts' which, in turn, will allow his second in command – the second man – to monitor the daily workload and the staff.

The second man has the task of delegating the daily jobs to each member of staff and ensuring that they are being carried out correctly. A second man needs to be all things to all people, having sufficient experience to take over in the stud groom's absence, the ability to motivate the staff – if necessary working alongside them mucking out or sweeping up – and being able to cope with the unexpected. A good second man will know the staff's strengths and weaknesses and will avoid allotting them tasks beyond their abilities, concentrating each one where he or she will be most effective. In order to enjoy a smooth ride, he will also need to identify potential problems among the staff. (A second man can, of course, be a woman – but I don't know of one!)

Stud hands come in all shapes and sizes, and both sexes. Some come straight from school, perhaps following in the footsteps of a parent. Some come from college or university on their way up the ladder to the manager's desk. Others simply love the idea of working with bloodstock but, for one reason or another, are not cut out for a job which involves riding. The duties of a stud hand require good general health and physical fitness. It would be foolhardy of a stud manager to employ someone who suffers from asthma or who has a history of back trouble. Some of the older stud hands still regard it a handicap to have women on the staff, but the girls are invaluable when it comes to handling temperamental mares or sick foals. They can also do a good job of keeping the lads in line!

Although the function of a Thoroughbred stud farm is to produce racehorses, the opportunity for stud staff to go to the races is as limited as for the average man in the street. There is little glamour attached to the endless round of mucking out, leading mares and foals backwards and forwards from paddock to stable and sweeping yards. Yet this labour-intensive business still attracts men and women from all walks of life to a job which starts at 7.00 a.m. and finishes when the last job is completed at the end of the afternoon. Weekends off are non-existent during the stud season; one day off at the weekend is usual – though, out of season, this lack of time off can be compensated for. The stud groom and second man rarely take time off between February and the end of May; they may have some quiet time over the weekends, but will always be on call.

Essential qualifications for working on a stud farm are a calm disposition and a sense of humour. Mistreatment of horses should never be tolerated from stud staff – it is a case for instant dismissal. Getting your feet trodden on, being kicked, having 10 tons of hay to unload fifteen minutes before you are due to go home, being called to a foaling when you have just stepped into a steaming hot bath on a cold February night – all this is good character-building stuff!

There is an effective 'grapevine' among stud staff, particularly in the Newmarket area where there is such a high concentration of stud farms. Not much goes on that the staff don't get to hear about. If someone loses his or her job through a major misdemeanour, they will have a hard time finding new employment within the industry. Likewise, marital or relationship problems are well documented, whether or not they have any foundation! A marriage that can survive Newmarket can survive anywhere.

There is an ongoing debate whether bloodstock breeding is a hobby or an industry. To own a few mares may well qualify as a hobby, but the business of standing stallions at stud is very definitely an industry. As in any industry, stud farmers have had to take a hard look at the economics of running a stud farm. One of the most obvious areas for savings is wages and many stud farms are now run with the absolute minimum of staff. Provided nothing major (such as an outbreak of disease) goes wrong fewer staff can, with the help of machines, get through the workload. A 'Bobcat' with a forked bucket can muck out ten stables in the same time it would take a man with a pitchfork to do two. A 'Billy Goat' blower can sweep a yard in half the time of men with brooms and a 'Terra Vac' can suck up more droppings in a paddock in one hour than a team of four shovelling them onto a trailer. Steam cleaning stables is now common practice; few people today believe it was once done with scrubbing brushes, elbow grease and Jeyes Fluid.

Even with the aid of machines, however, a normal day in the height of the season on a stallion stud is a physically exhausting experience. Take, for example, a stud with two resident stallions, each with 50 mares booked to him. A high percentage of the mares will have foals at foot and, while not all the mares will be resident throughout the season, those who do come to board will be stabled at night and turned out in the paddock during the day. Routines vary from stud to stud, but the average day will follow roughly the same pattern.

All the stock are fed by the stud groom or second man between 6.00 a.m. and 7.00 a.m., with checks being made on each individual for any abnormal behaviour or signs of ill-health. The full staff will begin work at 7.00 a.m., when 'teasing' commences. This will require the stallion man or his assistant to handle the teaser, the stud groom to observe proceedings and keep records and stud staff to lead a constant stream of mares up to the teaser one by one. Another member of staff will handle the foals while the mares are teased.

Next, the vet will arrive for routine work on perhaps a couple of dozen mares and several foals. The stud groom will be present to make notes, while one member of staff handles each mare and a second gives a hand with the foals. The vet, being busy, will not want to be kept waiting between mares, each of whom will require between five and twenty minutes of his time.

Meanwhile, those mares and foals not being seen by the vet can be turned out in their paddocks, which may be as close as a few yards or as distant as several hundred yards from their stables. Before, during or after the vet's rounds, one or more mares may be covered by the chosen stallion. While the stallion will be handled by the stallion man, at least two further members of staff will be required to handle each mare and, if a mare has a foal at foot, yet another member of staff will be required to watch the foal left in the stable. Since the stud manager, stud groom or a senior member of staff is required to witness the mating, liaison between all parties is essential.

Health and Safety Executive requirements should be adhered to throughout all procedures: information on antidotes for accidental contact with certain veterinary substances will be clearly displayed in each examination pen and hard hats will be worn in the covering barn to protect skulls from the flailing hooves of excitable stallions or nervous mares.

Once vetting and covering have been completed, the remainder of the mares and foals can be turned out, with special attention as necessary being given to newborn foals or sick animals. The veterinary examination room will require a thorough cleaning and, only when all these tasks have been completed, does breakfast figure on the agenda.

With the staff fed and watered, the mammoth task of mucking out can begin. Once the soiled bedding is removed from each stable and cleared away to a muck pit, each stable floor is swept clean and fresh straw is brought by tractor and trailer from the barns and properly laid in each stable. Hay will also be brought from the barn and distributed in each stable ready for the mares when they come in at night. Evening feeds are prepared: oats will need crushing and feed must be mixed and transported to each yard, ready to be put in each manger. As mucking out is completed, so the passage ways and yards will be swept and everything 'set fair'.

Once again, health and safety procedures must be adhered to throughout these processes: dust masks worn to protect against 'farmer's lung'; suitable footwear against the inevitable hooves stepping on human feet; hay and straw bales safely transported from barn to trailer, and trailer to stable; PTO shafts correctly encased on tractors; ear protectors worn and roller bars in place on the 'Bobcat'; ear protectors once more against noise levels when using the 'Billy Goat'; tetanus vaccinations up to date for obvious reasons.

A normal morning so far? Not any more. An owner has just arrived unannounced and would like to see both stallions and his two mares and foals. The professional stud farm will want to show the stallions groomed, with no sweat marks from earlier exertions; they will want to show the mares clean and tidy, with shining headcollars in a clean stable (it's raining and the owner cannot be expected to trudge across a wet paddock).

There are frantic radio/telephone messages to bring in the mares and foals (who have just been turned out) while the stud groom or manager shows the stallions in the stallion unit. Staff are dispatched to bring in the mares and foals who, delighted to be out in the paddock, show no inclination to be caught. Further members of staff are sent to help catch the mares, who are then bustled into clean stables. Both mares have rolled in the muddiest part of the paddock but no matter, headcollars at least can be cleaned. One headcollar breaks as the mare pulls back suddenly; a spare is frantically sought and cleaned. The owner is driven down to the stable yard; the car narrowly missing tractor and trailer laden with straw bales. As the owner is accompanied through the barn, an uninformed member of staff pushes a stable-load of soiled straw into his path; owner side-steps neatly in highly polished Gucci loafers – no sweat! The first mare and foal are brought into the central aisle for the owner to inspect; owner pats foal and gets bitten on the arm. Owner jokes about blood on his polo shirt. No sweat!

Owners should, of course, be welcomed at any time. Most will understand the nature of a working stud farm and will expect to encounter a workforce at full stretch. Nevertheless, an owner wanting to see the stallions and his two mares and foals involves a great deal of time and effort. To their credit, most owners appreciate the time and effort spent on their behalf and often leave a 'present', or tip, for the staff. These are gratefully received, are generally pooled and well spent in the pub at the end of the season.

Back to work. On a busy day, the stallions may have more mares to cover before lunch, which will mean bringing the mares and foals in from the paddock, 'dressing' the mares, rounding up the necessary members of staff, and turning the mares and foals out after covering.

Did someone mention lunch? The lunch break is generally taken at the same time each day, but it is not unusual for it to be interrupted by the announcement that an owner has arrived to deliver/collect/see their mare. They may be early or late for their appointed visit but the stud manager will want to create a good impression and the owner will not be expected to wait too long. Staff living on the premises will be summoned; living on the job can therefore be viewed as an advantage or disadvantage, depending on which side of the fence you are sitting.

The afternoon is spent completing any routine tasks left over from the morning. Setting fair the stables, distributing hay and feed to each box, sweeping up the yards. At peak times, mucking out can go on well into the afternoon – hardly surprising if there are a hundred stables! If the stallions have three mares booked to them in one day, the third covering will take place later in the afternoon, which means taking the stallion man and at least three other members of staff away from stable work.

Catching up mares and foals will start between 3.00 p.m. and 3.30 p.m. This may seem on the early side but, when you consider the time involved in catching and leading in up to 100 mares and perhaps 30 foals from various paddocks, it is understandable. Most mares will be eager to come in for their evening feed but once spring arrives, the grass is lush and the sun warm on their backs, there are always those who think it would be much nicer to stay out in the field. Once again. the 'posse' is summoned!

If this routine makes you tired just reading about it, consider the added factor of 'sitting up' – equine baby-sitting. Some stud farms employ staff solely for night duty; for instance a foaling foreman who is experienced in foaling mares and can be relied upon to deal with most foaling emergencies. Many studs, however, cannot afford this luxury and the stud staff work a rota for sitting up. The staff member works a full day, retires for a wash and brush up and a meal, then it's back to the sitting-up room at 8.00 or 9.00 p.m. until 6.00 a.m. the following morning.

The foaling boxes will be equipped with closed-circuit television so the stud groom and second man can keep an eye on any mare behaving strangely. One of them will be on standby throughout the night, so the sitter-upper can call them on a bedside extension when a mare looks ready to foal. Foaling records are filled in: what time the waters broke, what time the foal was born, when the foal first stood, and first sucked.

The sitter-upper will be relieved by whoever is doing the early morning feeds until the working day begins at 7.00 a.m. The sitter-upper will work the full morning and, apart from stopping for breakfast, not until lunchtime will relief come in the form of an afternoon off to catch up with sleep.

Despite the seemingly uninspiring nature of the job, a stallion stud can be great fun to work on. There is a sense of achievement with every foal who is brought safely into the world and every mare who is tested in foal. Once the flat racing season gets under way, every winner sired by one of the resident stallions is a feather in the cap. The stud farms whose stallions sire winners of the Classic races (the One Thousand Guineas, Two Thousand Guineas, Derby, Oaks and St. Leger) are given a great boost and courted by the media. This will cause a good deal of excitement

Delighted to be out in the paddock, showing no inclination to be caught

amongst the management, but will inevitably mean extra work for the stud staff. The manager will want to present photographers or camera teams with an immaculate establishment which, even on the best-run stud farms, will mean additional trimming, strimming and preening, with a lick of paint applied to any offending door or wall. It is not surprising, therefore, that the imminent arrival of the publicity machine is greeted with mixed feelings by the staff. However, the resulting press coverage in the daily nationals, the racing papers and the glossy racing magazines more than makes up for all the hard work. To be part of a successful operation whose achievements are publicly acknowledged gives rise to a huge amount of job satisfaction and pride. A labour of love? Yes – but a passionate affair!

A chapter on stud staff would not be complete without further reference to the position of stud secretary. It is undoubtedly a fascinating, all-consuming role, dealing with a huge variety of people and situations. Reading the racing papers each day may indicate an easy way of life but, when an owner rings up to find out how their mare is progressing, it pays dividends if you can congratulate them for having bred the winner of the 2.30 at Nottingham the previous day.

It is, however, a job that requires a great deal of self-motivation, since it is not unusual to be left unsupervised for much of the working day while the manager is out on the stud or has gone racing. Unless the secretary is one of several office staff, it will be necessary to be conversant with word processing, PAYE, VAT and basic accounting. A good knowledge of horses – preferably Thoroughbreds and stud work – will also be needed in order to be effective in the role. There are some other tasks that are unique to the job: posting small packages of fresh horse dung to the veterinary surgery for a worm egg count is one that springs to mind. Watching the racing on television is another – essential for keeping abreast of the stud's achievements!

The office is the focal point for all members of staff; the manager and stud groom will work closely with the secretary – who is often the person to whom other members of staff bring their problems. Since the majority of staff on stallion studs are men, a female stud secretary needs to be broad-minded. Not only will she comes across a great deal of sexual banter associated with the horses, she will also live with a predominantly male outlook on the world in general. An over-assertive female is not necessarily appreciated!

CHAPTER FOUR
POSITIVE VETTING

———•———

IN THE 'GOOD OLD DAYS' a mare would be sent away to the stallion stud where she would be teased, covered by the stallion every day she was in season and teased again at about 21 days. Then, if she didn't come back into season, she would be examined manually for pregnancy by a veterinary surgeon at around six weeks from her last covering date. If she didn't suffer any accidents or noticeable diseases, this pregnancy examination was probably the only veterinary experience she would have. Nowadays, things have changed. A glance at some veterinary records from the 1994 season shows that one single mare had 21 veterinary attendances between the end of February and early May. Another mare had just eight attendances. Both mares had been swabbed by a veterinary surgeon for contagious equine metritis and had blood samples taken to test for equine viral arteritis before leaving home.

The aim of a stallion stud is to get each visiting mare in foal as quickly as possible. To this end, studs quite rightly make use of the most up-to-date veterinary expertise at their disposal. This all costs money. A routine (shared) visit for a gynaecological examination, the taking of a uterine swab and smear and submission of these to the laboratory where aerobic culture and cytology takes place will cost around £25 plus VAT. A routine (shared) visit and a gynaecological examination alone will cost around £14 – and a mare may need up to six such examinations in one oestrus period to determine the optimum time for mating. The first-time breeder should therefore be prepared for a sizeable veterinary bill. This may be painful at the time but remember, the stallion stud and their veterinary surgeon will have your best interests at heart. For as long as the mare remains at the stallion stud, it is their job to do everything possible to get her in foal and, if this includes intense veterinary treatment, then so be it. They are the experts and should be left to get on with the job.

A veterinary surgeon specialising in Thoroughbred stud work is expected to be an equine gynaecologist, a fertility specialist, a paediatrician, an infectious diseases and virology expert and a dab hand with a needle and thread. Also, ideally, a diplomat, comedian, psychologist (equine and human) and the possessor of sufficient driving skills to proceed at breakneck speeds in the middle of the night on icy roads to arrive in one piece, with enough composure to deal with a difficult foaling.

Dedication is a pre-requisite of the veterinary profession. When did you last try (and fail) to get a doctor to call at your house in the middle of the night? A vet called at 2.00 a.m. will be there as fast as driving conditions permit. Furthermore, the vet will stay with a sick mare or foal until quite satisfied that the patient is comfortable, and will run the risk of being kicked, bitten or trodden on – a test of the best bedside manner!

Before the stud season gets under way, the veterinary surgeon will have taken stallion and mare swabs, administered routine vaccinations and rasped uneven teeth. There will probably be several stud farms to cover, so the vet will have completed many miles on stud work before the 15th February.

Swabbing the genital organs of a stallion is definitely a job for an expert. Some stallions take it in their stride but others will take exception to being interfered with. Administering a mild tranquilliser has the double effect of calming the horse and making everything 'hang loose', but may hinder the collection of pre-ejaculatory fluid. This however, is all routine procedure for an experienced stud vet and, on the whole, will present few problems. This is just as well since, before the stud season commences, each stallion will need to be swabbed twice, with swabs at least one week apart. Once the stallions have been given the all-clear from contagious equine metritis, klebsiella, pseudomonas and equine viral arteritis they will, if they are lucky, escape the attentions of the vet for a further six months. Not so the Thoroughbred broodmare.

Much of the veterinary work carried out on broodmares will require the vet's arm to be buried in their nether regions; the vet rarely sees the front end! It is the stud groom or manager's job to identify which mares the vet sees each day, and it is the vet's job to advise on the reproductive state of each mare and the optimum time for mating.

If a mare has poor vulval conformation or is showing signs of wear and tear after producing a number of foals, she may need a Caslick's operation. If the stallion stud informs you that your mare has been 'stitched' or 'sutured', it is this operation that they are referring to; it does not mean that she has gashed a leg and needed stitching. (That is not to say that accidents do not happen but, for the time being, we will stay in the region of reproductive organs.) The reason for stitching is to close the gaping parts of the vulva to prevent faeces and other debris going where it should not. Local anaesthetic is administered, a fine sliver of each vulval lip is taken off and the lips are stitched together. By exposing the flesh, the stitched lips will then heal together, after which the stitches can be removed. It is a routine procedure, but its success will depend to some degree on the quality of the stitching. Some vets are so ham-fisted that the two sides are dragged together too tight, giving inadequate stitching no chance of holding. Vets with a more delicate touch will produce no strain or stretching, and stitch so neatly that you wish they had been around to stitch you up after your appendix operation.

One veterinary surgeon's wife was so impressed by her husband's talent with a needle and thread that he was given the mending to do at home on a permanent basis. She was also an enthusiastic rider to hounds and, following in the car one day, her husband was summoned to her aid. 'Can you manage a few stitches?' she asked her husband. He looked round the horse but found no sign of a cut. Then his wife dismounted and, sitting on the grass verge, opened her legs to reveal a split seam in her breeches. Stitches having been hurriedly but neatly applied, she remounted her horse and rode confidently back to the hunt!

Once a mare has been stitched, it is essential to make a note of it in her records. Mares who have been 'stitched low' (had a lot of stitches) may need to be 'opened up' before they are covered, and re-stitched afterwards. The following year, stitched mares

He will run the risk of being kicked, bitten

will need opening up again before they foal to avoid the risk of tearing as foaling commences. As grisly as this procedure sounds, it is done in the best interests of the mare and causes her little or no discomfort.

When the mare is showing in season to the teaser, she will be subjected to a gynaecological examination and a cervical swab and smear by the vet, who will continue to monitor her and will advise on the optimum time for mating. If the mare has a poor breeding record or has proved difficult to get in foal so far, she may be given semen extender before covering. This is a solution which is inserted into her vagina to create the best possible conditions for the semen to live for the longest possible time.

Once the mare has had a clean swab and smear report and has been covered, she will be examined yet again by the vet to determine whether or not she has ovulated. If not, she will be covered again by the stallion and the examination process will continue until ovulation is seen to have taken place. If she has a positive swab and smear report, she will need a course of treatment before anything else can be done. Some of the the more common 'bugs' to be found on a cervical swab are beta haemolytic streptococci, alpha haemolytic streptococci and E. coli. These may sound life-threatening, but are usually disposed of by administering the correct antibiotic.

Scanning mares for pregnancy will start as soon as the first mare to have been covered reaches the 16 day stage, or the stage at which the stud normally carries out a first scan. Everyone – including the veterinary surgeon – will be eager to have the first mare scanned in foal. If you have never seen an ultrasound scanner photograph before, it is not very helpful to have one arrive by post without explanation. At this early stage, on a positive scan, a 'black hole' will be identified. This is the fluid-filled foetal sac; solids show up white, fluids black. While the foetal sac will be of recognisable size at this stage of pregnancy, it can still be confused with uterine cysts, which are also fluid-filled. A mare who is pregnant will also have good uterine 'tone', whereas a mare who is not pregnant may be in the early stages of coming back into season. If there is any doubt at the first scan, the mare may be scanned again two or three days later, to double check. A mare thought not in foal at 16 days can surprise everyone when a foetal sac pops into view on the scanner picture two days later!

The second scan, approximately 28 days after mating, will determine whether the 'black hole' is a normal pregnancy by whether it has increased in size and by the detection or otherwise of the beginnings of a foetus and a heartbeat. A manual examination and a third scan at about 40 days will clearly show the foetus, which will have increased in size, and should pick up the healthy beat of a heart. A further manual examination and scan are routinely carried out at about 60 days.

The tricky moment is when twins are discovered. Very few mares carry twins successfully to full term and, if they do, one is often too weak to survive. Added to that, there is a higher risk of complications at foaling so, unlike sheep, it is preferable for horses not to carry twins. With the help of the ultrasound scanner, a twin conception can be detected as early as 16 days and, where the foetal sacs are in separate 'horns', the task of removing one is relatively simple. The veterinary surgeon simply pinches one sac, which is usually sufficient to cause its disintegration. This procedure is more difficult when the foetal sacs are lying side by side. However, daily monitoring by scanning can often find them drifting apart, which allows access to the smaller of the two. Although a twin *may* dislodge without veterinary help, the longer twins are left, the harder it is to deal with them, so it is usually worth taking action sooner rather than later.

It is one opinion that uterine cysts can, if abundant, hinder the early stages of pregnancy. One mare was known to have several large cysts. She was covered and conceived, but was not able to maintain her pregnancy beyond 25 days. She was covered again and the same thing happened, so it was decided to send her to the Equine Fertility Unit at Newmarket. There, they have specialist laser equipment to 'zap' the cysts and, in this case, it proved effective. On close examination, the mare was found to have a cluster of large cysts on one central stalk. Once the stalk was cut, the cysts were flushed out and the mare returned to stud, where she was covered, conceived, maintained her pregnancy and produced a healthy foal the following year.

In order to carry out gynaecological examinations and minor surgery in safety, stallion studs will have an examination pen constructed, otherwise known as the veterinary 'crush'. This device is far removed from the cattle crushes seen in Herriot country; the modern horse crush will be situated within a large stable or custom-built room, much as an operating table in a hospital theatre. It will be copiously padded and have a non-slip floor. Hot and cold water will be on tap in the room and electrical points will be conveniently situated for the scanner. The examination room will have a fridge, stocked with a supply of antibiotics and other medicines which, with regard to health and safety regulations, will be securely stored. Raiding the fridge will turn up no end of delights: semen extender, frozen colostrum, and a variety of chemical hormones. Other standard supplies kept in the examination room include copious amounts of gamgee and cotton wool, wormers by the dozen, arm-length plastic gloves (usually yellow or blue) and the essential Lubrel, a lubricating gel for gloved arms in readiness for internal examinations.

Like doctors, veterinary surgeons can sometimes be accused of talking over the heads of lay persons, in a language that seems completely alien. One owner was understandably concerned when he received an invoice for treatment of 'submandibular lymphadenitis' in his foal. He was quickly reassured when this was translated as a cough and sore throat. The best vets will explain in layman's terms exactly what they are doing, why they are doing it and what they hope to achieve. One cannot then complain about 'plain speaking'; we are, after all, talking about sex – albeit equine – and there are only so many words to describe reproductive organs and their functions.

When you consider that much of a veterinary surgeon's time on a stud farm is spent looking at and exploring the nether regions of horses, you will appreciate the need for a sense of humour. Veterinary banter is not for the squeamish or shy; much double entendre comes into play and it can be painful to watch a teenager, fresh to the workplace, have his or her sexual habits verbally explored by the vet, who is really just trying to make the youngster feel part of the team.

The health and safety regulations applicable to certain drugs commonly in use on a stud farm can give rise to much speculation, as can the use of X-ray equipment. Pregnant women should not assist when X-rays are being taken and a veterinary surgeon can have a lot of fun at the expense of anyone who does not fully understand the reasons why.

'Any of you girls who had sex last night should leave the room', announced a mischievous vet, portable X-ray machine at the ready. The girls remained, giggling, but the vet had noticed one of the lads turn a shade pinker.

'Anyone who has had sex in the last week should leave the room', came the next ultimatum. The lad became more agitated as the girls carried on giggling. The vet proceeded to X-ray the mare's leg and, when he had finished and the girls had gone, he noticed the same blushing lad hanging around.

'Everything OK?' enquired the vet.

'I had it two nights ago' stuttered the lad, 'will I be all right?'

In addition to carrying out routine work on mares, the veterinary surgeon will need to attend newborn foals and any other foals who are off colour. Newborn foals will have a course of antibiotics and tetanus antitoxin injections at birth to reduce their susceptibility to infection. They are, after all, delivered in a stable full of straw, some of which will inevitably be soiled; neither a sterile nor a natural environment.

Minor surgery at stud is not always directly concerned with reproduction. A foal may be born with an entropion eyelid, which means the eyelid is turned in, with the lashes trapped against the eye. A delicate touch is needed to roll the lid out and stitch it back lightly until it heals in the normal position. A month later, you wouldn't known there had been anything amiss.

On stud farms where mares and young foals share a paddock in their early days it is advisable to make sure that each one can be correctly identified. Every Thoroughbred is issued with a passport, in which is recorded the white markings and whorls (hair partings) peculiar to each animal, along with sex, date of birth, parentage, name (once given), record of vaccinations and any official endorsements (changes of ownership or country of residence). The markings of each foal are therefore recorded by a veterinary surgeon, who will then issue a markings form which is incorporated into the passport. For means of identification among foals, markings can be taken between 12 and 24 hours after birth. Mares and foals have been known to get mixed up and, although each individual is parentage-tested in due course by means of blood-typing, the sooner an error of this nature is rectified, the better for all concerned. Even though they have been completed and signed by a veterinary surgeon, markings forms should always be checked carefully, both for accuracy of the content of the form and for accuracy when checked against the foal. Even experienced vets have been known to inadvertently change the sex of a foal – much to their embarrassment!

Descriptions of markings should also be checked carefully; if you look at the diagram the vet has to complete to match the written description, you will see how easy it is to transpose the 'fore rear view' (also captioned *anterierus vue posterieure*) and the 'hind rear view' (*posterieurs vue posterieure*). Every written description is, of course, different but a typical one will read like this:

HEAD: Irregular triangular star inclined right of median. Contained whorl on upper eye level right of median. Non-contained whorl on upper eye level left of median. Small snip at lower nostril level.

NECK: Crest whorls mid both sides of neck, left lower than right, both have feathering to poll. Whorls mid ventral mandibles.

L.F: No markings. Whorls posterio lateral forearm.

R.F: White medial and posterior coronet. Whorls posterio lateral forearm.

L.H: White to fetlock extending above anteriorly.

R.H: White to fetlock.

BODY: No markings. Whorls both stifle folds. Whorls both axillary folds with feathering above.

With such detail, accompanied by a diagram, it is possible to identify each individual without recourse to other means, such as branding. Even when a horse has no white markings at all, the number and position of each whorl will be unique to that individual. Recently, veterinary surgeons have been asked to include drawings of the 'chestnuts' on these markings forms.

These are the horny extrusions found on the inside of each leg, slightly above the knee or hock. Every single one is different and, if a method could be found to 'fingerprint' these chestnuts, it could, indeed, be a foolproof means of identification.

Weatherbys, whose role is described more fully in the next chapter, have strict guidelines for veterinary descriptions of markings, and recognised abbreviations for colour and sex. 'Male' and 'female' may sound correct to you and me, but it is strictly 'colts' and 'fillies' for foals. One young veterinary surgeon insisted on placing squares with crosses and circles with arrows in the box for 'sex' – which wouldn't do at all!

Determining the colour of a foal is not always easy. The majority of grey horses are born with dark coats, either very dark brown, bay or chesnut. (Incidentally, the colour chesnut is *not*, according to Weatherbys, spelt with a 't' between the 's' and the 'n', despite the Oxford Dictionary listing.) However, if a foal is eventually going to turn grey, there will be some grey hairs around the eyes and muzzle, so the vet's description will be bay/grey or chesnut/grey. Horses who are destined to be grey will take a variable time to 'turn'; some will be grey throughout their coats by the time they are one year old, others will take three or four years to turn fully.

If, when visiting a stud farm, you see a foal with a bulge under the tummy, towards the hind legs, it will probably be an umbilical hernia. These, though unsightly, often give no trouble but, if they continue to get bigger, they can become 'strangulated'. The operation to repair a hernia is quite straightforward and will usually entail a 24 or 48 hour stay in 'hospital' before mare and foal are allowed home again.

Colt foals have a narrower pelvic opening than fillies – much the same as in humans. Occasionally, colt foals have difficulty passing their very first droppings (the 'meconium') and will need an enema. In severe cases, where enemas fail to work, the foal will require an operation to have the blockage physically removed. It is always a little nerve-racking to operate on very young foals but, if the operation is quick and efficient, there is every chance of success.

Sick foals are always a worry, both to the stud staff and the veterinary surgeon. Very young foals, in particular, have limited resistance to virulent bugs and can deteriorate very quickly indeed. Vigilance is half the battle – a foal who is slightly lethargic or simply not looking as bright as the others should be checked with the thermometer and watched very closely. Veterinary advice should be sought sooner, rather than later.

A young foal who 'scours' persistently can go downhill very quickly through a combination of the infection causing the scour, and dehydration. The vet will use a stomach tube to administer extra fluids, and antibiotics will be injected to fight the infection. In addition, a binding agent can be used. A local branch of Boots was at first alarmed, then full of concern, when two dozen bottles of a proprietary brand of diarrhoea medicine were ordered post-haste when a number of foals went down with same bug!

A foal whose resistance is lowered can also become suscep-tible to chills which, in turn, can deteriorate into pneumonia. It is therefore vital to keep the foal warm and, in addition to a warm, dry stable with plenty of clean straw, it may be necessary to put a rug on the patient. Foal rugs are obtainable from good saddlers but a lambswool sweater with the sleeves cut off can do the job just as well!

Nursing a sick foal is a round-the-clock job. A veterinary surgeon may be required to attend the patient on several occasions throughout the day and night but, in between visits, the foal may need to be helped up to suckle, watched for any change of symptoms and generally made comfortable. A good mother is a blessing; a 'foal-proud' mare or a bad mother can be a real trial for the foal and the handlers, and may need a mild tranquilliser.

On a stallion stud with perhaps a hundred visiting mares, the veterinary surgeon can expect an intense period between the busiest months of March and May. It is normal for the vet to visit every single day during that period, and to spend anything from one hour to more than two hours coping with the workload. There will, of course, also be other clients to see, and perhaps late evening emergencies and night calls to a foaling. Despite all this and although, in theory, the work on one large stud could be shared, it is preferable for the same vet to attend the stud throughout the season. In this way, continuity is achieved. While two vets may diagnose the same clinical symptoms in a sick animal, the one who has been attending throughout will be in a much better position to assess the animal's rate of improvement or deterioration.

Such continuity is also useful – although not foolproof – when a mare is being examined daily to assess her preparedness for breeding. Especially in this context, it is worth remembering that, whenever a veterinary surgeon gives an opinion, this is what it is – an opinion. Such an opinion will be a thoroughly informed, professional judgement, based on knowledge, experience and on the symptoms or facts available. However, while a mare may show all the clinical signs of being ready for mating, if she is not teased, you will not know whether she is really ready until she is presented to the stallion. Furthermore, there are mares who, although clinically in a fit state to be covered over a period of three or four days, will only stand for the stallion on *one* of those days, when Nature decrees that the time is right. Attempting to cover her at any other time will bring out the devil in her, endangering the handlers, the stallion and even herself. This does not mean that the veterinary surgeon is anything other than *technically* correct, but Mother Nature has not relinquished all responsibility. The vet may be positive but, when a mare says 'no', she is the one who is right!

CHAPTER FIVE
BREEDING BUREAUCRACY

W HEN IT COMES TO RACING and breeding, you would be forgiven for wondering who was in control of what. Pick up any racing paper or magazine and you will find reference to the British Horseracing Board, The Jockey Club, The Jockeys Association, the Racecourse Association, The Racehorse Owners Association, The Levy Board, Tattersalls, The Thoroughbred Breeders' Association and Weatherbys.

In 1993, things took a turn for the better when the newly formed British Horseracing Board (BHB) became the governing authority for British racing. The Jockey Club, which is not a club for jockeys, but an institution founded in the eighteenth century that traditionally ran racing, has not become obsolete but retains its role of regulating racing. The Jockeys Association *is* an association for jockeys and The Racecourse Association *is* an association for racecourses. The Horserace Betting Levy Board, to give it its full title, distributes the levy, collected through betting, to racing – though not nearly enough of it. Tattersalls Ltd. is the major British sales company specialising in Thoroughbreds. The Thoroughbred Breeders' Association (TBA) is the body that represents the interests of Thoroughbred breeders, its voice being heard on the BHB through that body's Industry Committee.

The organisation with which the breeder will have most contact is Weatherbys. Based at Wellingborough in Northamptonshire, Weatherbys Group Ltd. is appointed by the BHB to carry out the administration of racing. Weatherbys are also proprietors of the *General Stud Book* and have a department which is responsible for all the administration involved in registering each individual Thoroughbred.

Sending a mare away to stud will generate a great deal of paperwork. By the time the mare's first offspring has reached the racecourse, no end of official forms will have been filled in. If they haven't, it is possible that the horse will not even be allowed onto the racecourse, let alone to run in the race. The Rules of Racing are strictly adhered to and any horse without 'papers', duly signed and sealed correctly with the required proof of vaccination, will be a non-starter.

There is, then, a lot of seemingly incomprehensible small print attached to owning or breeding a Thoroughbred. Rather than becoming hugely frustrated in an effort to understand it, you may find that a telephone call to the TBA or Weatherbys Stud Book Department pays dividends. They will explain each process in plain English, and you will sail through it all without a hitch. If you are a member of the TBA, you will have an opportunity to visit Weatherbys and see how it all works. Even if you are not, Weatherbys operate an open door policy and welcome small or large groups of enthusiasts.

Breeding a single Thoroughbred will require a broodmare application form, a covering certificate, a markings form, a registration form and an assortment of veterinary tests and certificates. A markings form is also known as an FIC (foal identification certificate) or an FID (foal identity). To register a foal you don't have a foal registration form but a mare return form; a compilation of all mare returns is called the *Return of Mares.*

A covering certificate ('Certificate of Covering of Mare') is the official confirmation of a mating. A covering card, on the other hand, is notification of mating but has no official status. A foal cannot be registered unless you have the covering certificate from the year of the foal's conception. Parentage testing by analysis of a blood sample is also required before registration can be completed.

Much confusion is traditionally generated through both the mare return form and the certificates needed to accompany it; the covering certificate and the markings form.

'Can you send me my covering certificate?' came a familiar request from an owner on the telephone.

'The certificate for Blossom was sent, let me see, yes, last November – the 12th to be precise – to your home address.'

'Can you remind me what it looks like?' asked the owner.

'Last year they were pink, and it's about 8" x 7", with the name of the covering stallion, your mare's name, passport number, breeding, first and last service dates and your name and address on it.'

'I thought they were green', said the owner.

'They were green the year before, pink last year and they are yellow this year', I replied patiently.

'Well, what colour is the one I'm after?'

'Pink.'

'With the foal's date of birth?' the owner persisted.

'No, it's the covering certificate for *last* year and your foal was only born *this* year.'

'Right. Pink you say?'

'Yes, pink.'

'OK, I'll get the wife to have another look for it. Cheerio!'

Later the same day, Blossom's owner rang back.

'I've found the covering card', he announced.

'The covering certificate? Good, as long as you've got it.' There was more:

'Now then, where do I fill in the foal's details?'

'Those go on your annual mare return form.'

'Mare return form?'

'Yes, that's also a pink form, with your mare's name on it, the covering stallion for last year and a space for the foal's details.'

'Right. So I don't need to send the covering card off.'

'Yes, send them both off, together with the markings form.'

'I *do* need to send them both then?'

'That's right, along with the markings form.'

'Markings form? What does that looks like?'

He got there in the end; Blossom's foal was duly registered and issued with a passport. If you board your mare at someone else's stud farm, they may offer to carry out the registration procedure for you, thus enhancing the service they offer.

Identity cards for humans may be a thing of the future but a

Sending a mare away to stud will generate a great deal of paperwork

Thoroughbred horse cannot do anything of importance, in or out of his country of birth, without a passport. Every Thoroughbred born in Great Britain or Ireland must be registered in the *General Stud Book*, and is issued with a passport. To qualify for registration and to guarantee the purity of the breed, both the sire and dam must also have been registered, tracing back to the *General Stud Book* or the approved foreign equivalent.

To begin at the beginning, a broodmare is not officially a broodmare and a stallion is not officially a stallion until their passports have been stamped GONE TO STUD by Weatherbys. At the next stage of proceedings, each mare mated with a Thoroughbred stallion is issued with a covering certificate, which is the official confirmation of that mating. It will show first and last service dates, the mare's name, passport number, the name of her sire and dam and the name and address of her current owner. The certificate has a signed declaration by the stallion owner or his representative that the mare's passport was examined, her identity verified, that the covering was a 'natural service' and the mare was not inseminated artificially. 'Natural service' is defined as 'the physical mounting of a mare by a stallion **and** which can include the immediate reinforcement of the stallion's service or cover by a portion of the ejaculate produced by the stallion during that service or cover of that same mare'.

Immediate reinforcement by a portion of the ejaculate? Refer to your veterinary surgeon for a delicate enlightenment! It is also interesting to note that a foal is not eligible to be registered in the *General Stud Book* unless 'a natural gestation took place in and delivery was from the body of the Mare in which the Foal was conceived' and that 'No Foal which was conceived by artificial insemination or which was the subject of an embryo transplant can be registered in the *General Stud Book*.'

Weatherbys send each stallion owner a 'book' of numbered covering certificates for each stallion, which are filled in at the end of the season with each mare's particulars. The counterfoils, containing the same information as the certificates, are returned to Weatherbys who then produce a 'broodmare listing'. This form is sent out to all owners of registered mares at the end of the year. It lists each mare owned and contains the covering information received from the the relevant stallion owner. Weatherbys ask for confirmation of the result of mating, that is to say whether the mare is barren (not known to have been pregnant), aborted early (was certified pregnant at 40 to 50 days, but was later tested empty – or does not have a foal so resorption/abortion is assumed) or slipped (certified pregnant after covering but aborted after 5 months). Since the definition will affect the stallion's fertility statistics, it is important to be specific. If the mare is barren it may or may not be the fault of the stallion. If she aborts early or slips, the stallion has done his bit, so the mare should be included in the number of mares he got in foal that year.

Included in the information on the broodmare listing is the last date of covering. Once this has been confirmed by the owner, Weatherbys will know approximately when the following year's foal will be over one month old. From this information they can, in due course, issue a blood-typing kit to each owner of a mare due to foal, staggering the dates to protect the Animal Health Trust in Newmarket from being inundated with gallons of blood at any one time. Weatherbys do occasionally have hiccups. One owner, resident in Hong Kong but with mares boarded in England and Ireland, received six blood-typing kits at his Hong Kong office, much to the consternation of his secretary there. (A note here for worried postal workers: each blood sample is secure in its padded polystyrene labelled container, and the whole kit is sealed in a plastic bag inside the envelope before posting.)

As mentioned earlier, a veterinary surgeon will issue a markings form for each foal, usually soon after birth, but before the foal is four months old. This is sent to Weatherbys in due course. However, the blood sample required for parentage testing cannot be taken before the foal is one month old. Weatherbys will then send each mare owner a mare return form (also referred to as an 'annual return'), which lists each mare and their respective covering stallions for the previous year. Once completed, this form is sent back to Weatherbys with the relevant covering certificates, markings forms and registration fees – every transaction being charged for. So long as there are no discrepancies in the paperwork, the foal's passport will be dispatched to the owner, who will be asked to check it for accuracy.

Mares who are temporarily imported to Great Britain to be covered by a stallion, and who produce a foal while they are in Great Britain, should be included on a 'foreign mare return,' either by the owner's agent or by the stallion stud that the mare is visiting. This return is much the same as the normal mare return, but includes the phrase 'Foals entered on this form should be only those *dropped* in Great Britain or Ireland by visiting foreign mares . . . ', which may explain the weathervane at the National Stud – a stork carrying a foal.

When is a horse's passport not a passport? Since Weatherbys changed its name to a 'document of description' (DOD). This contains the animal's date of birth, colour, sex, country of birth, sire, dam and maternal grandsire. It also shows the breeder (who may be different from the owner), the *General Stud Book* reference (e.g. Vol. 43 *General Stud Book*), the passport number, and confirmation that the animal has been parentage tested. It bears the official stamp of the issuing authority which, in the case of Great Britain, is Weatherbys Group Ltd.

In the *General Stud Book* is the list of country codes: the internationally agreed suffixes used to denote the country of foaling when names are registered for animals foaled outside Great Britain. Thus, the suffix (IRE) denotes an animal born in Ireland, and (FR) tells you that the horse was born in France. I wonder whether there is a Thoroughbred born in Jamaica named *Strawberry* (JAM) or a Kenyan-bred *Big Red* (KEN). You could have a Moroccan *Just A Bit* (MOR), a Norwegian *Neither* (NOR) or perhaps a *Lived In* (SIN) born in Singapore!

Naming a horse may sound fun but, when you consider that in Volume 42 of the *General Stud Book* alone there are over 23,000 mares, and then add the named produce in that volume you do not have the choice you may have imagined. Nonetheless, you can have a great deal of fun thinking of names based on a foal's sire and dam, a pertinent anagram or something such as the well publicised one recently in use, *Jafeica* – which apparently stands for 'just another f . . . . . . expense I can't afford! There are supposedly strict guidelines for naming horses: no offensive language for example, though there are some dodgy-looking anagrams and spoonerisms about! No more than 18 characters including spacing and punctuation can be used, but you can run two or more words together or spell phonetically – for example *Letsbeonestaboutit*.

Scanning the *General Stud Book* at random turned up some well named horses: *Ebb and Flo* by *Forlorn River* out of *Dam N'Blast*; *Intimate Guest* by *Be My Guest* out of *As You Desire Me*; *Report 'Em* by *Staff Writer* out of *Correlative*; *Integrity* by *Reform* out of *Cry of Truth* and *Valiant Vision* by *Brave Invader* out of *Sweet Dreams*. With so many horses in Middle Eastern ownership, there are also some curious names in existence: *Fattaanah*, *Mawaal Habeebee* and *Wasslawayeh* for example!

By the time a mare's first produce has reached racing age, her owner will have built up a substantial file for her and her offspring. For a stud that stands two stallions, each with an average of 50 mares booked to him each season, the record-keeping is a mammoth task. Add to that the complete history of each resident broodmare and you will understand why computers figure high on the modern stallion stud's list of requirements.

When the owner of a mare applies to send her to a stallion, the stallion stud will first ask for particulars of that mare. If, for instance, there is only one nomination left to the stallion, the mare's age, pedigree and breeding history will be among the deciding factors. Once the mare has been accepted, her owner will be sent a nomination agreement (contract) for signature and a pre-covering record to be completed in detail. Both must be returned to the stallion stud before the mare arrives there. Once a mare's booking is confirmed, the stallion stud will need to check that the veterinary certificates for EVA and CEM are negative, ensure they have been dated within the required time, and place them on each mare's file for easy reference. Approximate arrival dates will be booked forward in the diary, and details of foals born prior to arrival at the stud will be noted.

On arrival at the stallion stud, each mare's identity is checked against her passport, which is also scrutinised for vaccination records. Unless they have been received in advance, veterinary certificates and swab reports should be checked before the mare is allowed off the horsebox. Any bumps or scrapes suffered by the mare and/or foal on the journey should also be noted.

Checking a mare's identity on arrival at the stallion stud is essential. Checking her identity before she *leaves* for the stallion stud is equally important! One Norfolk farmer had booked his mare to a stallion who stood at a stud 70 miles away. He brought the mare in from the field, loaded her on the horsebox and drove for two hours to the stallion stud. When he unloaded her, the stud groom took her passport, checked her markings and stood, scratching his head and muttering.

'Is there a problem?' enquired the owner.

'We'll have a hard job getting this in foal', replied the stud groom.

'I can't see why, she's got a good breeding record.'

'Your *mare* might be a good breeder, but this is a gelding!' The owner turned a deep shade of pink as he looked between the animal's hind legs. He didn't live that one down for a while.

If a blood-typing kit for the foal is sent with the mare, the dates during which the blood samples are due to be taken should be booked forward in the diary – it is so easy to put the kit on a shelf and forget it until it is past its 'use by' date. Late blood samples can, unless you have a good excuse, incur a penalty charge from Weatherbys.

If the mare is sent to the stallion stud in advance of foaling, her owner will want to know how she is progressing, particularly if she goes past her due foaling date. Once she has foaled, details of her foal and any problems will be relayed to the owner. Many stallion studs now take a polaroid photograph of the foal; few owners have time to visit their newborn foals, particularly if they live at the opposite end of the country.

The stallion stud office will be constantly updating their list of mares booked to each stallion and, as they receive further details of the mares, they will compile stallion charts listing the numbers of barren, maiden and foaling mares, and a foaling chart listing the in-foal mares and their expected foaling dates. An excellent working book, which can hold a huge amount of information on each mare visiting the stallion, is *The Thoroughbred Breeders' Association Stallion Management Daily Records*. The information stored can include the name of the owner, the mare's age, colour, sire, dam, her last service date and which stallion she is in foal to. In addition, it has spaces for the passport number, the date each passport was received and dispatched, the date the foal markings form was sent to the owner and the date the covering certificate was sent. Whether a mare has aborted or slipped and whether she was stitched on arrival and/or departure can also be recorded.

In a further section you will find a page per month, divided into date squares. This is where you find noughts and crosses and other strange hieroglyphs! The standard shorthand of a teasing chart is as follows: 0 means the mare has been teased but is not in season; X means the mare was teased and found in season; ♂ can mean she was teased and may be coming into season while ♀ can mean she was teased and is not quite but almost teasing out of season. S means she was served, and OV on a single day means she has ovulated. On the other hand, O and V on consecutive days could mean she was teased not in season and was seen by the vet (V) the next day! Scanning is usually abbreviated to the number of days from service that the mare was scanned, with a tick for positive or Neg. for negative. Depending on the user, we may well find a period that reads like this:

0 0 0 0 0 X X S X S X ov 0 0 0 0 0 0 0 0 0 0 0 0 0 0 0 18+

Or, less satisfactorily:

0 0 0 0 0 X X X X S X S X S X S X ov 0 0 0 0 0 0 0 0 0 0 0 0 0 0 18Neg X X S X S X ov . . . and so on.

A covering card or letter will be sent to each owner on each occasion that their mare is covered, and a scanning card or letter will inform them of a scan result. (In addition to sending photographs of newborn foals to owners, many stallion studs now send the ultrasound scanner photographs, showing each stage of the pregnancy. These make a novel change from showing baby photographs over coffee.) With the increased use of fax machines it is possible to cause a degree of confusion with too much information too soon, unless you include 'if' and 'but' in your communications, go into minute detail, or are prepared to furnish the owner with daily bulletins. Mares can make bigger fools of you than women!

All the time, veterinary reports will be gathering in the mare's file. She will already have a negative CEM swab report on file, together with a negative EVA test result. To this will be added the results of any blood tests, and of the worm egg count, taken to ensure that she isn't 'wormy'. (Most stud farms worm each animal once a month, but resistances can build up and extra worming may be required.) Each mare who foals will have a 'foaling record', containing details of the foaling and a copy of the foal markings taken by the vet. Copies of all letters or faxes sent to the owner will be added to the file, together with a regular foal report produced by the manager or stud groom, which monitors the general progress of the foal.

The stallion stud will invoice each owner for the keep of their mare and foal on a monthly basis, and will issue their nomination invoices in June (for 'straight fee' nominations) or September (for '1st October' nominations). Both the keep and the nomination will, in most cases, carry VAT, but owners do have the option of registering for VAT – if they want to enter the realms of VAT returns.

An owner venturing into the breeding industry for the first time would do well to become a member of the Thoroughbred Breeders' Association. The main object of the Association is 'to encourage by means of the provision of educational or research facilities or otherwise the science of producing and improving the Thoroughbred horse in Great Britain'. It also strives to 'ensure co-operative effort in matters pertaining to the interests of the breeding of Thoroughbred horses'. Although the executive and office staff are salaried, the president, chairman and those constituting the council of the association volunteer their services. Despite the good works that emanate from its offices, the TBA is frequently shot at from all directions; for not doing enough, for doing too much, for having too little power or attempting to wield too much. It's a case of not being able to please all of the people all of the time – but they do try.

However, leaving the politics to one side, there are many advantages to be had from paying £60 a year to become a member of the Association – not least receipt of the monthly racing publication, *Pacemaker & Thoroughbred Breeder*. This – unless you are sufficiently excited by reading Europe's top bloodstock magazine – has nothing to do with stimulating the heart muscles. If you want to find out more about the TBA, they are always happy to meet prospective new members at their offices in Newmarket, and you can combine a visit there with an afternoon's racing at racing's 'Headquarters' – as the town is fondly known.

As administrators of the *General Stud Book*, Weatherbys are able to produce a great deal of information about the Thoroughbred population. *The Statistical Record*, which started life as *The Statistical Abstract*, is published by Weatherbys in conjunction with the TBA and the Irish Thoroughbred Breeders' Association. Opening *The Statistical Record* annual for the first time will probably give the impression of 'just a lot of figures' but, once you start looking in earnest, there is an incredible amount of fascinating information. From 'Leading Sires in Order of Total Money Won', through 'Winning Distances of Sires' Progeny' to 'Analysis of Return of Mares' – if you want a statistic, this is your book! There is a pretty foolproof guide on 'How to Use *The Statistical Record*' at the beginning of each volume, and it does pay to read this before you start wading your way through. This is, by its own admission, unique among racing publications. It links the performances of racehorses to their parents, tracing stud careers of mares and listing the successes of a stallion's progeny, to be compared to other stallions. Statistics are not limited to the equine species; the records of breeders are now featured, with a new statistical table which lists breeders by the success of their progeny!

CHAPTER SIX

EXPECTANT OWNERS

———•———

THERE IS NO SUCH PERSON as a typical racehorse breeder. Her Majesty the Queen, Middle Eastern Princes, pop stars, politicians, farmers, carpet consultants and housewives are all listed racehorse breeders. What they have in common is the desire to breed a winner. Disposable income is the only requirement, and even that is not necessarily needed in great quantity. True, it is more desirable and satisfying to own your mares outright, but racing clubs are abundant and many of them include a breeding programme in their package. You may find you only own .01 per cent of a broodmare, but you can still have a lot of fun.

Those who can afford to invest in more than one mare will usually make a decision at the outset whether to breed to race or breed to sell. 'But if we are breeding racehorses', I hear you say, 'then surely everyone is breeding to race'. Quite right. The significance of the term 'breeding to race' is that the animal you have bred remains in your ownership, at your expense, when transferred from stud to the training establishment. Breeding to sell means breeding with the intention of selling the progeny, usually at public auction, either as a foal or a yearling. There are many compromises: racing the fillies and retaining the better ones to build up the broodmare band; selling all but the best bred colts; selling only the best bred colts. One good foal or yearling sale in a year will often make the difference between whether or not you can afford to keep and race some of your stock the following year. If, on the other hand, you keep and race them all and have luck on your side, you may win a tidy sum in prize money and then sell one or more of the winners for an even better price as a valuable stud animal. Of course you could keep them all, at great expense, and find that none of them has that star quality.

Clearly, making such decisions is far from easy. There have been many occasions when the ugly duckling has proved to be a swan on the racecourse – after being sold at a loss as a yearling. Conversely, the pride and joy (both on pedigree and looks) that you keep and pay all those training fees for could just as easily turn out to be slower than a riding school hack. This is one of the fascinations of breeding – there are no certainties.

Owners of large numbers of broodmares will either keep them on their own stud farm or board them en masse at a boarding stud. Owners of very large numbers of mares may even board them at several stud farms in more than one country. Such owners will employ a bloodstock manager, or managers, who will oversee the whole operation. The stallion studs who receive the support of these owners will probably communicate manager to manager or even secretary to secretary. From a purely practical point of view it would, for example, be impossible for the Queen to visit each of her mares at each stallion stud during each season.

Film stars and pop stars can be found among the ranks of registered breeders, but are well disguised. It took me two years to realise that a certain gentleman who had sent his mare three years running to the stud where I worked was, in fact, Englebert Humperdinck. Similarly, George Michael is not actually called George Michael and his stud farm is listed under his father's name, so you need to know someone in the know before you know it's him! When it was suggested to one stud manager that the mare owner would be better known to him as George Michael, it still rang no bells.

'You know,' he was prompted, 'the singer, George Michael.' The stud manager, unfamiliar with teenage idols, was none the wiser.

'What does he sing?'

'He's a pop singer', replied the incredulous agent.

'Oh, you mean a banjo player!'

The House of Lords is well represented among racehorse

breeders – hardly surprising when you consider that racing has its foundations in the realms of gentlemanly wagers by the upper classes. Their lordships and, indeed, their ladyships have invested heavily in the racing and breeding industry, developing famous racing bloodlines from the foundations laid by their ancestors. In contrast, there are also many ordinary people whose love of racing and breeding has led them to invest in a single mare. If you are a keen amateur golfer or sailor, your hobby will cost you a considerable amount over the years you choose to indulge. Investing in a broodmare will certainly cost a considerable amount in initial outlay and maintenance, but think of the possibilities – just one good sale or an exceptional winner could recoup a considerable amount, and there is always the chance of a dream come true in the form of a top class colt being sold to take up stud duties.

British racing remains the envy of the world, with its variety of courses where the vast majority of races are still run on turf. Each racecourse has its unique bends and undulations and is subject to the vagaries of the British climate, resulting in going that can be 'hard', 'heavy', or anything in between. The Epsom Derby is undoubtedly the most prestigious race for a breeder (or owner) to win, despite being run over what some consider to be an unconventional course, full of cambers, gradients and turns.

In recent years, the British racing and breeding industry has benefited from massive Middle Eastern investment, but the involvement of the Arab owner-breeders is met with mixed feelings. While they were building up their breeding operations they spent huge sums on yearlings, to the benefit of many breeders whose stock would otherwise have sold well, but not *that* well. Now that they have established their breeding programmes, they are not so active in the yearling markets, and they may perhaps seem to win more than their fair share of races, big and small, from Royal Ascot to Thirsk on a bad day.

However, if the Arabs pulled out of their British operations overnight, there would be a gaping hole in the industry, leaving many stud owners and trainers wondering where the next penny was coming from. With such vast numbers of horses, they cannot accommodate them all at their own stud farms, and so board their mares at a number of stud farms throughout the country. They employ numerous managers, assistant managers, independent advisers, office workers and stud workers – not to mention trainers and their staff. They also sponsor races, research and racing charities. Long may their robes flow around the English turf!

Those owners who have the time to manage their own breeding operations will derive great pleasure from formulating breeding plans for their mares and following the resultant offspring throughout life onto the racecourse. This entails choosing stallions and visiting studs, seeing newborn foals, weaning and taking care of youngstock, watching a two-year-old learn to gallop with a lad on board and, finally (hopefully), cheering as the youngster fights for the lead up the home straight. Disappointments will come thick and fast, but it's all worth it when your first winner comes in!

At the stallion stud, the mare owner is the customer and is therefore always right. Or not? As any stockbroker will tell you, there is a downside as well as an upside to investment. When that investment takes the form of unpredictable equines, you need more than your fair share of luck to come out on top of the game. Provided that you satisfy yourself that a stallion stud is run on sound principles of horsemanship and husbandry, you should have no reason to complain to them if your mare ends the season not in foal. Sadly, there was a case recently of an owner attempting to sue a stallion stud because his mare ended the season not in foal, and with a uterine infection. If every hopeful parent sued their gynaecologist on similar grounds there would be an outcry. There would, in all likelihood, be perfectly sound medical reasons for both the parentless state and the infection, neither of which could be attributed to the professional involvement of the expert.

Fortunately, the vast majority of owners are indeed happy to trust in the professional judgement of the stallion stud management, and will put the unproductive years down to experience. Those owners who have a bad run and still appreciate the efforts to get their mares in foal are, in themselves, professionals. They may have firm views on how a stallion stud should do this or that but, on the whole, their opinions are respected.

With such a wide variety of owners' occupations, stud staff receive some unusual presents from those delightful breeders who take a little extra trouble. One of the best gifts I received was from a couture marketing company who, delighted with the polaroid photograph of their newborn foal, dispatched a token of their appreciation. Naturally, it was addressed to the stud office which, on this occasion, meant that delivery was to the stud owner's house. He was not a happy man when, having been up for a 2.00 a.m. foaling, he was woken by the postman at 6.00 a.m. to sign for a recorded delivery parcel containing a deliciously sexy selection of stockings!

Another eagerly awaited, regular end-of-season parcel was from a dairy owner. Butter, cream, cheese and cheese spreads were shared out between the stud and office staff – diets went out of the window and the mare probably got an extra bowl of oats! Badger Bitter from the West Country was another 'thank you' present, as was a hand embroidered make-up bag. The stud groom didn't think much of the latter, but he had few other complaints. Each Christmas he was sent a goose and a duck from a regular client and received half a lamb, jointed and ready for the freezer, from a sheep farmer who grazed his stock on the stud.

As one stud season draws to a close, so the mare owners will start thinking about mating plans for the following year. Once an owner has made a shortlist, you would think that the next step would be to visit the relevant studs and inspect the stallions at close quarters. In reality, relatively few owners make this visit, which always puzzles me. When you send your mare away to stud, you are not only investing in the stallion fee, you are also placing your mare and foal in the hands of that stud's management for up to several months. Of course, the best studs will be known by reputation to be up to the mark, but there is no substitute for visiting the premises, meeting the manager or stud groom and the staff, and satisfying yourself that it is a well run operation.

Some breeders prefer particular stallions for the least logical reasons; colour can play a major part. A strong colour is nearly always preferred, for example a bright chestnut rather than a 'wishy-washy' colour – or a deep, dark bay. One gentleman carried out lengthy research into the extent to which a particular grey stallion passed on his colour. He then went 'shopping' for a mare who contained specific colour lines in her pedigree and booked her to the stallion, just to produce a grey for his wife, who wanted only grey racehorses. He certainly produced the right coloured animals; unfortunately, they were not very fast!

And then there is the question of size. It is quite usual for an owner to ask how big a stallion is, particularly if their mare is very big or very small. So I was not in the least taken aback when a customer rang, without giving his name, to say he was interested in sending his mare to one of the stallions, but wanted to know how big he was.

'He stands 16.1 hands high', I said.

'Right. But how big is he, dear?'

'He's 16.1', I repeated.

'No, no. You see my mare's not so big and I don't want her hurt. How *big* is the 'orse?' The penny dropped.

'He's no bigger than usual', was all I could think to reply.

'Go on with you, don't you know?' came the leery voice.

'May I ask again who is calling?' The line went dead.

For some breeders, temperament is another deciding factor. This can, of course, be determined by the way a young horse is handled, and some trainers are noted for getting the best results with a certain type of temperamental horse. However there are some stallions whose offspring appear to be more flighty than others, or who show a tendency to bad temper. Since a horse's attitude can be the make-or-break factor on the racecourse, some would consider it folly to mate a mare who has always been bad tempered with a stallion who has a reputation for being nasty.

The experienced breeder will recognise the difference between an exuberant stallion and a nasty one but, to the inexperienced, a fit, virile stallion can display worrying tendencies.

'I've just passed the stallions out on exercise. Is it safe to take them out like that?' asked one worried visitor. She explained that, as she had driven past the end of a public right of way, she had seen one of the stallions bucking and kicking, with his man looking decidedly worried. She had stopped her car and got out, to be met by the stallion roaring like a bull elephant and trying to bite his man – who was cursing like the devil. Thinking better of it, she had got back in her car and come straight to the office. It transpired that two little girls on ponies had just ridden past in the opposite direction and one of the ponies had been very obviously in season. The young girl rider had tried to hurry past but her pony mare, quite overcome by the prospect of the advancing stallions, had frozen to the spot. This particular stallion, who was accustomed to covering any mare who was presented to him in such a delectable state, was not at all happy about being led past, and his man was rightly agitated at the little girl's inability to get out of the way. He was in complete control and the stallion soon settled – but not before the visitor had seen him behaving outrageously.

Stud farms are, by their nature, lovely places to visit. Newmarket holds a veritable feast of delights for the mare owner – who would need a week to visit all the stallion studs properly. Outside 'Headquarters', stud farms are to be found throughout the country and can make a pleasant day out for the family, although dogs and babies are not necessarily welcome.

One Turkish family who were frequent visitors to a stud farm where I worked were delighted to hear that I took a close interest in the newborn foals. They obviously thought I had maternal longings and arrived one day complete with newborn baby. As usual, they were invited into the office and, to my horror, the baby was ceremoniously placed in my arms.

'You lika the bambinos, yes?' I was lost for words. 'You cradle the bambino now and we come back later.' Not quite what I had in mind!

Then there was the lady with the Old English Sheepdog who, handsome as he was, seemed to think he was a foal. His owner would walk along the stud drive and the dog would squeeze under the fence, loping across to a group of mares and foals. To the foals, who had never seen anything like him in their short lives, he appeared as a four-eyed green monster. They shot off in all directions, their mothers undecided whether to join them in flight or tackle the culprit. The dog's owner eventually whistled him back, explaining that he often trotted around the paddock with her mares and foals at home; she didn't seem to appreciate that, whereas her foals had probably seen the dog every day from birth, he was an 'orrible sight to those who saw him for the first time.

With the stud season under way, some mare owners will visit the stallion stud to see their foals. Newborn foals often have weak joints or crooked legs which, in time, will strengthen and straighten. However, for an inexperienced owner, it can come as quite a shock to see a photograph of one or more seemingly crippled legs – and they will hasten to the stud to see for themselves. The difference a week makes is extraordinary: 'But that's not the same foal you sent me a photo of', retorted one owner. He had, he said, been gravely concerned on receipt of the photograph which showed both front fetlock joints almost touching the ground. The foal had quickly strengthened, the fetlocks were all but normal – and the same filly went on to win three races.

When it comes to sending their mares to stud, owners can be economical with the truth. 'Can be a little foal-proud' was the comment on one mare behaviour form. The stud staff were experienced and, although the mare showed signs of temper when they handled her and her foal, she didn't cause any undue concern. The owner was informed the following morning that his mare had foaled.

'Everything OK?' he asked casually.

'Yes, mare and foal have settled nicely', he was told.

'Mare behave herself, did she?' the owner pressed.

'Yes she did. A little foal-proud – but you'd told us that, so we were careful.'

'That's all right, then. It's just that she kicked our stud groom out of the stable last year – put him in hospital with a fractured leg.'

Similarly, a mare was delivered to stud one day in May with a request from her owner that she should live out at grass and not be brought in at night. 'She settles better like that', added the owner. The mare was put into a stable on arrival so that a dung sample could be taken before she was turned out. She was obviously upset from the journey and unhappy to be stabled, sweating freely, walking round and round the box and whinnying incessantly. It was a warm spring day and, dung sample collected, she was duly turned out in the field where she settled immediately with several other mares. She proved quite difficult to catch but, with sufficient staff and patience, was caught as necessary for teasing, vetting and farriery and was, in due course, covered by the stallion. The owner was sent his covering card, and telephoned as soon as he received it.

'You managed to catch her then?' he asked.

'Yes, she's not the easiest to catch but we've managed.'

'That's amazing', he said; 'it took six people half a day to catch her to come to you, and then she jumped a hedge into the next field before we got her. She gets claustrophobic see. Put her in a stable and she goes right barmy, so we leave her out in the field with a shelter.'

Cash flow is as important to a stallion stud as it is to any business. When owners send their mares to stud, those mares need feeding and the feed bills need paying. The staff, farrier and vet all need paying for their services. Invoices for 'keep' charges, though sent out monthly, are frequently paid late, while stud fees due to be paid on 1st October can take several months to arrive. The majority of owners do pay well, but those who do not quickly make a name for themselves. Despite this, many stallion studs continue to take bookings from them, on a promise of 'I've got things sorted now, payment won't be a problem this year'. Stallions who are struggling to produce good results may have difficulty attracting mares. Applying the theory that the more mares he covers, the more foals he'll have, and the more chances on the racecourse, a bad payer will still represent one more mare for the stallion.

When non-payment gets out of hand, it is not unheard of for a stallion stud to 'claim' a mare and make what they can out of her. First catch your mare! If the owner has run up a sizeable bill without paying a penny, it is not unreasonable to ask for payment before the mare can be taken away by her owner. Owners do not think much of this, but they usually pay up. Once a mare has gone home to her owner, getting her back is tricky!

Then there are those who like to pay in cash. Big wads of notes. I did have a panic attack one morning when a large sum of cash in a brown envelope was discovered on the office dormat with just the invoice number written on the outside. Opening the package, I recoiled at the sight of what looked distinctly like blood on several of the notes. Checking the invoice number hurriedly against the customer list, I was relieved to discover that the notes had come from an owner who happened to be a butcher!'

One of the best mare owners I ever had the pleasure of dealing with was often ahead of the billing system, bringing his cheque book to the office and asking me to write the cheque out for whatever he owed in the way of keep for the month. He was always the first to pay his nomination fee and never complained when keep fees or stud fees were increased. A rare phenomenon in the business world today.

Sadly, open sentiment is not often encountered in the racing and breeding world. Occasionally, when a star emerges, owners, trainers and jockeys will be moved to tearful adoration – and quite right, too. Among the professionals of the stud world, people who plainly regard their mares as 'one of the family' are frowned upon, with no justification whatsoever. It was, therefore, one in the eye for such cynics when a leading, titled breeder was so thrilled with a particular foal that a birth notice appeared in a leading daily national newspaper: 'To Mrs. Moss, a son . . .'

New owners should be welcomed with open arms by all sections of the racing and breeding industry, and actively encouraged. Sadly, people who have little or no knowledge but who are keen to learn are often dismissed out of hand by those 'experts' who cannot be bothered to explain the basics. How many times have I heard the response 'God, that man/woman knows nothing!' when a new owner has had the misfortune to say the wrong thing. If no-one has explained that it is beneficial to put a barren or maiden mare under lights from December onward, how is a novice supposed to know? Where does a new owner start?

Although the TBA has its knockers, by becoming a member you will gain access to a vast bank of acquired knowledge. Not only will you have access to a comprehensive library on breeding a racehorse, you can, in theory, start by contacting your area representative and picking their brains. One thing will lead to another. You will pretty soon find the helpful individuals who are prepared to take time and educate you.

Provided that you have consideration for those establishments who are working flat out during the stud season or during intense sales preparation of yearlings, you can arrange visits to any number of public studs, take part in seminars for stud owners and managers and talk to any number of experts on veterinary matters, nutrition, paddock maintenance, pedigrees, and even how to lobby your MP on matters pertaining to breeding and racing. When you take the plunge, buy your mare and send her away to stud, do not be afraid to ask if you do not understand something. If you cannot get a reasonable answer to a reasonable question, say so! If all else fails, send your mare elsewhere the following season.

People who plainly regard their mares as 'one of the family' are frowned on, with no

CHAPTER SEVEN
STARS IN THEIR EYES

———•———

B EAUTY, THEY SAY, is in the eye of the beholder. In the case of the potential racehorse, beauty is dependent upon the potential to gallop quickly. At the bloodstock sales where potential flat-race horses are auctioned, you can take it as read that all those on offer will have been bred to win; whether they have been bred to do so over the minimum distance of five furlongs or the maximum of two and a half miles, is a matter of pedigree.

There are three principal bloodstock auction houses in England: Tattersalls Ltd. at Newmarket, Doncaster Bloodstock Sales and Ascot Bloodstock Sales. Of these, the most prestigious is Tattersalls, whose annual Houghton Yearling Sale offers the crème de la crème of Thoroughbred yearlings. That does not mean that stars cannot emerge from Doncaster or Ascot. *Lyric Fantasy*, who won all her four races and £92,077 as a two-year-old was sold as a yearling at the 1991 Doncaster St. Leger Yearling Sales for just 12,500 guineas. (It is one of those curious eccentricities that bloodstock in England and Ireland is still sold in guineas. In America it is dollars, in France it is francs, in Germany it is deutschmarks, but the guinea still reigns supreme for bloodstock sold in England and Ireland. If achieving a single currency in Europe is a tall order, doing away with guineas at these bloodstock sales would surely be well-nigh impossible.)

Park Paddocks is the home of Tattersalls in Newmarket. Anyone can go to a sale there – it is a public auction. Yet the outsider is given the distinct impression that it is hallowed ground, where only the chosen few may tread. There are certain

Beauty, they say, is in the eye of the beholder

places within the sales ring where it is traditional for 'regulars' to stand or sit and a newcomer would be well advised to ask before making himself or herself comfortable on a seat from which can be seen every angle of the ring; its occupants and their potential purchasers.

Heaven help anyone who stops for a chat in front of a bidder at a crucial point in the proceedings. Although this is understandable from the bidder's point of view, some of them do disguise their actions so completely: how are you to know that the man with his *back* to the auctioneer, chatting to someone in the row of seats above him, is twitching a finger at the auctioneer behind his back! The stairs and the 'gate' (where the horses come into the ring) are also prime spots for bidders, so don't hang around there trying to make polite conversation. You would also do well to refrain from passing judgement while a Lot is being sold – or at least from doing so out loud. 'Look at those dreadful hocks' is not the sort of comment a vendor wishes to hear as the bidding is about to start. *He* may know that the animal has dreadful hocks – but there may be a man there who doesn't!

Walking around the sales complex at Newmarket, you will see in an instant the varying degrees of professionalism. Regular sales consignors will have pedigree boards decked out in the racing colours of the breeder, or in their own familiar colour schemes. Staff will be in matching 'uniforms', and tubs of flowers will mark the rows where their horses are stabled. The horses' coats will dazzle you with their shine; every whisker will be trimmed; every mane pulled to uniform length. Burnished buckles on bridles will be matched only by the glint in the eye of the salesman.

Doncaster has a much more relaxed atmosphere about it, with less 'hype' and more in the way of good, plain speaking. It is also colder – but it's a cheaper place to buy a cup of tea and a sandwich than Newmarket. Doncaster is where the round of yearling sales starts, with its St. Leger Yearling Sale held early in September. The first day of the sale will usually have a morning session, and this will be followed by three evening sessions on the next three days after racing. These evening sessions, whether at Doncaster or Newmarket, have a very special atmosphere which is an essential experience for the would-be breeder.

At Ascot Bloodstock Sale, neither the same number nor quality of bloodstock passes through the ring but it is, nevertheless, a useful market for a certain type of animal. To put the three auction houses into perspective, the results of the bloodstock sales held in Great Britain in 1995 were as follows:

Auction House	Lots sold	Aggregate (gns.)	Average (gns.)
Tattersalls	3,864	75,508,905	19,541
Doncaster	2,788	14,272,365	5,119
Ascot	981	2,000,578	2,039

If you are a racing fan, you will find yourself bumping into many of the 'stars' of BBC or Channel 4 racing, especially at Tattersalls. Trainers will be shopping for owners; owners, from the one man band to the rich and famous, will be be buying or selling; commentators and journalists will be there to keep an eye on the proceedings. Many jockeys have an active interest or involvement in breeding; some of their equine partners may also be seen passing through the ring en route to new ownership or to a stud career. The sales scene at Tattersalls is a cosmopolitan affair. Americans, Japanese, Italians and Germans are now joined by Eastern Bloc buyers, complete with film crews to chart their progress. To illustrate the extent of international trade, at Tattersalls 1993 Horses In Training Sale, buyers came from 22 different countries.

Once you have got the auction dates from, say, the TBA, you can telephone the auction house and ask them, as a potential purchaser, to send you a catalogue for their forthcoming sale. You may be asked if you are interested in just the yearling sales or if you would like your name added to their mailing list. Go for the mailing list – this way you can build up a library of catalogues, containing hundreds of pedigrees, which could be useful reference for the future.

When your catalogue arrives, put on a powerful pair of spectacles and read the small print. Whether all vendors and purchasers do this I do not know, but it is advisable if you do not want a nasty surprise later in the proceedings. In particular, read the lengthy explanations of 'wind examination'. These do not refer to flatulence but to the presence or absence of 'abnormal inspiratory sound' – in plain terms, whether the horse has any respiratory problem that might affect racing ability.

And so to the pedigrees themselves. Each page containing, for example, a yearling pedigree will state where the yearling has come from directly to the sale. (Owners who do not have the facilities or the expertise to prepare yearlings for sale will sell their yearlings through a professional consignor – probably a stud farm or an agent.) The name of the actual owner may or may not appear next. This information will be followed by a note of where the animal will be stabled at the sales complex; if you refer to the map in the front or back of the catalogue you will be able to find where each animal is without the need to walk the whole complex in ever-decreasing circles. Next will come a brief description of the animal, for example: 'A BAY COLT, Foaled March 3rd 1994'. If the animal is the first produce of the dam it will state: (first foal). After the Lot number is a declaration of whether or not the animal is being sold with VAT – a cost difference of 17.5 per cent, depending on whether or not your bloodstock dealings are registered for VAT. Then comes a tabulated pedigree, showing three generations of the sire and dam. So far, so good. Next comes the hard part!

Stallions qualify to stand at stud by virtue of their pedigree and their racing performance. Some qualify on one count alone, or at least have a weakness in one area, It may be that one is closely related to a top class racehorse with a top class pedigree but has failed, either through inability or an accident, to notch up any success on the racecourse. Another may have proved a tough, consistent performer on the racecourse, but have a weak pedigree. Either way, parentage and achievements will have been well documented, and a summary of each stallion is included either on the page containing the yearling's pedigree or in a section at the front of the catalogue.

The page containing the yearling's pedigree will always detail the dam's line: the breeding records of the first three dams, and the winners they and their daughters have produced. In the front of a Tattersalls catalogue you will find a 'Guide to Cataloguing Details', which explains in some detail how the pedigree is laid out and the relevance of 'black type' in that pedigree. In the back of the same catalogue will be a list of all 'Group' and 'Listed' races run in the UK in the relevant year; since the status of races does change from time to time this is a useful reference to keep you up to date.

The Guide also explains which typeface represents which class of race. For example bold capitals denote the winner of a European Pattern race, a Foreign Graded Stakes race, a Listed race or a Major American Stakes race, while bold upper and lower case denotes a horse placed in any of those races. This does, however, assume that you know what these descriptions mean. In very simple terms, racing in Britain is graded from top to bottom, with the Pattern races (Group 1, Group 2 and Group 3) at the top of the tree. Foreign Graded Stakes are, broadly speaking, the equivalent of the British Pattern races – although Group races in some countries are not regarded so highly as those in the UK, Ireland, France and the USA. Group 1 races carry the most prestige and the most prize money. They include, for instance, the Derby, Oaks and St. Leger, and races such as the Coral-Eclipse Stakes and the Haydock Park Sprint Cup Stakes. The next level is Group 2, then Group 3, followed by Listed races. In the catalogue, other races are simply referred to as 'races', the total winning value of which may or may not be included – for example 'won 2 races and £4433 at 2 and 3 years'. National Hunt racing (steeplechasing and hurdling) has a similar system of grading but, for the purposes of a flat-race pedigree, any reference to an animal's racing performance refers to flat races unless otherwise stated.

From this you will see that a pedigree containing a lot of black type is a better winner-producing family than one with very little. Compare the difference between the pedigrees of yearlings in a Houghton Sale catalogue and those in a St. Leger Sale catalogue. The yearlings in the Houghton are the top of their year and their pedigrees will contain much black type in their first, second and third dams, leaving little space for any information on earlier generations. In the St. Leger catalogue there will be less black type early on in the line, so you will find many pedigrees containing extensive detail of fourth, fifth and even sixth dams. There is lengthy, ongoing debate among experts about the relevance of a pedigree beyond the first three dams. There is also much debate about the rights and wrongs of breeding pedigree to pedigree without having due regard to the conformation of the individuals concerned. It is certainly worth taking the time to read all the arguments as you will undoubtedly glean a lot of knowledge; breeding is a fascinating subject which will continue to be hotly debated. (The one thing that most pedigree experts would agree on is the unpredictability of Thoroughbred breeding. Just because a 'star' has been produced by mating a particular mare with a particular stallion, there is no guarantee that mating the same two animals again will produce a similar result.)

Once you have a basic understanding of what you are looking at in a catalogue, it is time to go to your first sale. Start with a yearling sale. Here you will get a feel for the business, see who is buying what, and also make some notes about yearlings by stallions who take your fancy for the mare you intend to buy later in the year. On the other hand, you could start the other way round: buy a yearling filly to race at two and three, and then retire her to stud.

You will be equipped with your catalogue which you will, of course, have studied in minute detail from 'Conduct of Sale' to 'Complaints Procedure' and 'Drugs', in addition to scrutinising the pedigrees it contains. If you start with the St. Leger Yearling Sale at Doncaster, you should sport a warm set of clothes, topped by a suitable hat and tailed by a warm pair of socks under a comfortable pair of shoes. No high heels (you will be on your feet all day), no three-piece suits, no children under five and no dogs.

If you go with an expert, whether breeder, stud manager or bloodstock agent, keep asking questions. Get them to point out the good and bad points of each animal they see. If you are serious about buying a horse, then you will have a short-list of those which interest you most and which you believe will come within your price bracket. Find out where each of your 'possibles' is stabled and ask the attendants to walk the horse up the concourse and back so that you can assess the movement. If the consignor is there, ask him or her any questions that spring to mind.

They will all tell you that their colt or filly is 'a star' or 'just the ticket' and is 'sure to win a race for you'. But of course! No matter that the animal is back at the knee, splay-footed and has one clubby foot. These are some of the points that a bloodstock agent may bring to your attention, but will they mean anything to you? Probably not. Ask your expert for a specific opinion of the horse's legs, feet and overall conformation and to explain why any faults are either undesirable or acceptable. If any terms are used that you don't understand, always ask for an explanation.

A good judge of a horse will look at each animal as a whole, weighing up the importance of any shortcomings. A perfect horse is a rare creature indeed, but there are those whose shortcomings are so minor that it is reasonable to assume they will not affect the horse's ability to race. The first impression a horse gives will often be the true one; a horse who possesses real quality, shows lots of 'presence' and moves fluently in a balanced way can be forgiven minor defects.

A horse's action when he moves is of great importance. Good, sloping shoulders are very important in the Thoroughbred, as this is where the low, fast action comes from. Although some animals move badly at their slower paces and well at fast paces, or vice versa, there are some defects that will come into play no matter what the pace. Having said that, it has been proven many times that a horse who has defects and moves badly may, nonetheless, be able to gallop fast, while a near-perfect horse may show no ability at all.

This is a vital point for those who set out with the intention of breeding purely to race. Don't despair too soon if your youngster looks like a gangly teenager, shuffling along and tripping. The important point is the gallop. Once the youngster has grown up a bit, been broken in and started work on the gallops, you may be pleasantly surprised to see your gormless teenager shaping up as a promising athlete. (If, conversely, you are breeding to sell, you will be anxiously watching each stage of development, and will become extra critical of each animal. The rate of development may well be the deciding factor in determining whether to sell an individual as a foal or as a yearling.)

Immediately before going through the sales ring, each animal will be walked around the outer ring with several others, waiting their turn according to their Lot number. From time to time you will see a horse led out to a covered area at one end for a closer examination by a potential purchaser and/or his appointed veterinary surgeon. This will give them an opportunity for a final check before they decide to bid for the animal, but it can also give rival bidders a chance to see who they may expect to be bidding against. Small groups will be seen huddled in conversation, nodding, shaking their heads, consulting their catalogues and muttering into mobile telephones. Other groups will be extolling the virtues of the horse they are selling in an effort to attract an extra bidder. Last minute consultations between owners and agents will centre on just how much they are prepared to spend: 'Is that your top price, or would you go another thousand if pushed?'

Once you have acquired a good basic knowledge of what you are looking at, both on pedigree and conformation, it is time to take a seat overlooking the sales ring. The auctioneer will be on his rostrum, hammer in hand, while above him will be displayed the Lot number being sold and the sum that is being bid for that Lot in a variety of currencies: sterling, Irish punts, US dollars, French francs, Italian lire, etc.

There are traditional spots around the ring for regular buyers – not least the bank of bloodstock agents, who will want to watch who they are bidding against. Then there are the 'spotters', in the form of attractive young ladies, strategically placed around the ring looking out for fresh bidders. If you take a fancy to one of the spotters, make sure you don't start your chat-up line whilst bidding is in progress – it could be expensive!

Watching for bidders is fascinating. Although it is not as obvious as following the ball at Wimbledon, heads will swivel to watch for the next move: will he go an extra 1,000 guineas, an extra 5,000? The real drama starts when the 'big guns' go for the choice animals and bidding, after reaching 200,000 guineas, goes up by 10,000 guineas a nod.

Telephone bids are also taken. Now that a mobile telephone seems to be an essential accessory of the sales 'uniform', bids come in from as close as the surrounding stable areas, or even from the bar! You will sometimes see a 'link-up', with an agent outside talking to the client on the telephone, listening to the bidding and giving the nod to a colleague to bid on, or to stop right there.

The auctioneers display a real art in selling the wares on offer. Each has his own 'patter' and, if you shut your eyes, you would easily be led to believe that the horse in the ring at that moment is *just* the one for you! They tease out the bidders, tantalise them with suggestions that it's a 'sure thing' they are passing over: 'Just one more time, sir. You can't let the other chap take this one from you!'

At some point, you will hear the term 'pinhooker'. I have no idea where this term originated from, but it refers to those people who buy foals with the sole intention of re-selling them at a profit as yearlings. This is not so easy as it sounds. Quite apart from the fact that you need to keep the individuals alive and well for the best part of a year, the success or failure of the other progeny of each foal's sire can make or break a transaction of this kind. An example of successful pinhooking was the filly foal who was sold at public auction in Ireland for just 1,900 guineas only to be sold for 190,000 guineas as a yearling to the Arab-owned Gainsborough Stud! In the meantime, the filly's sister had won the Group 1 Fillies Mile at Ascot, just a week before the auction, thus becoming acknowledged as one of the best two-year-olds in training.

If you buy a foal by a sire who has his first runners the following year, and that sire goes on to be leading first-crop sire, you will, if your foal/yearling is in one piece, stand an excellent chance of selling on well. Always remember, however, that this scenario is not that likely, and it will have cost you a considerable sum to keep and prepare the foal for sale as a yearling. A risky business then, but one which has paid dividends to those who are blessed with that happy combination of shrewd judgement and luck.

If, when you have seen how the system works at a yearling sale, you are still keen to invest in a mare, Tattersalls December Sales is a good shopping place. The first day is dedicated to yearlings, and is followed by several days when foals are sold. The last week is when mares, plus fillies and colts out of training, are sold as breeding prospects.

The catalogue containing mares' pedigrees will be much the same as the yearling catalogue, with the obvious additions of a line stating whether a mare is in foal and, if so, to which stallion she is 'believed' in foal, and what her last service date is. Every in-foal mare will have a covering certificate lodged with Tattersalls, and will have been checked for pregnancy shortly before the date of the sale. Each mare's breeding history will be documented on the pedigree page and this, together with her pedigree, age and covering sire, will determine her value. The British Bloodstock Agency produces a guide for purchasers, listing what they believe each mare will sell for. This is extremely useful as, although you may easily pick out half-a-dozen mares you would like to buy, they may be well out of your price range.

It is important to decide at this stage what type of stock you are aiming to breed. If you are hoping to breed a Derby winner, you will need to spend a lot more money on a 'Classic' pedigree than if you are aiming for a good two-year-old sprinter. Breeding speed to speed should, in theory, produce more speed – but this is not necessarily so. A racemare who proved slow over a mile, mated with stallions who were bred for and won over a mile, may produce more slow milers. Sending the same mare to a sprint-bred stallion might inject the extra speed needed to produce a winner over six or seven furlongs – or even the mile. It is all part of the fascination of breeding!

When buying a mare, taking an expert with you can pay dividends. An expert who has been around the stud scene for a while is likely to know many of the vendors and the mares they have on offer. What may seem like a bargain could be on the market for any number of reasons. Although the breeding record is there on the page for you to see, she may be a difficult mare to get in foal, she may have a bad temperament, or she may have consistently produced foals with bad legs.

A bad horse costs just as much to keep as a good one, so aim as high as you possibly can. It is better to go home empty-handed than to buy just any horse for the sake of it. A seventeen-year-old barren mare who has bred nothing of note is not the kind of start you should be looking for, no matter how attractive she is. If you need to compromise, it is better to go for a maiden filly, who has perhaps won a modest race. If you have done your homework and studied your maternal grandsire list, you will know which of the proven sires in this field to look out for – but then so will everyone else!

The bars and restaurants in the sales complexes are always fertile places for gossip. Since they are inevitably crowded places, overhearing other peoples' conversations is unavoidable at times. It pays to remember this if you want a private conversation! There is a monitor in each bar telling you which Lot number is being sold and how the bidding is going, so you won't miss anything.

If you are undecided about whether to take the plunge and invest in a mare, going to the sales as an observer can be just as much fun. If you combine the Doncaster St. Leger race meeting with the St. Leger Sales, racing at Newmarket with the Houghton Sales or the Stallion Show and Trade Fair at the National Stud with the December Sales, you will be sure to find all the key players around. You will also find bloodstock agents and stallion managers ready, willing and able to take nomination applications for the following season. What is more, if you don't buy a horse at the sales, someone is quite likely to offer you the 'real star' they have tucked away in their stable at home!

CHAPTER EIGHT
WINNING WAYS

———•———

THERE IS NO DENYING that the more you spend on quantity and quality of mares, the better chance you have of breeding a good winner. However, not only is it possible for owners of just a few mares to breed winners; it is possible for them to breed winners of good, or even Classic races.

Mister Baileys, 1993 winner of the Two Thousand Guineas, was bred by Mrs. Gibson-Fleming, who had just three broodmares. *Thimblerigger*, the mare who produced *Mister Baileys*, was purchased in foal at Tattersalls December Sales in Newmarket for 22,000 guineas. The resulting offspring, by the stallion *Nishapour*, was sold as a foal for 10,000 guineas. Mrs. Gibson-Fleming then sent the mare to *Robellino*, a stallion standing not far from her own stud farm. The result of this mating, also sold as a foal for 10,000 guineas, was purchased by owner-breeder Paul Venner as a companion to another weanling at home. Although the *Robellino* youngster was sent to the sales as a yearling, there was little interest in him and Paul Venner decided to put him into training. The rest, as they say, is history.

Mister Baileys won three races as a two-year-old, including the Group 3 Lanson Champagne Vintage Stakes, before going on to win the Two Thousand Guineas at three. He then went on to run a scintillating race in the Derby, finishing fourth and taking his total prize money to £271,527 into the bargain. A half share in *Mister Baileys* was bought by the National Stud at Newmarket, where he was due to take up stallion duties in 1995 at a fee of £6,500. The highs and lows of owning horses were clearly illustrated when, with breeders queuing up for his services, he was struck down by grass sickness – often a fatal condition. The subject of an insurance claim, he was purchased by Vinery Stud in the USA, where he is set to take up stud duties in 1996. So far, he has had no recurrence of grass sickness.

At fifteen years of age, *Thimblerigger* was already in the autumn of her breeding life when she produced *Mister Baileys*, and she was sold privately after he was born. Mrs. Gibson-Fleming is said to have no regrets about selling *Thimblerigger*. It was her decision to send the mare to *Robellino*, she owned the mare when *Mister Baileys* was born and she will remain in the record books as the breeder of a Classic winner.

Although Jeff Smith cannot be termed a small breeder, the story behind the nation's favourite racemare, *Lochsong*, must surely give heart to all aspiring breeders. Having had horses in training for eight years without hitting the heights, Jeff Smith purchased a big, black yearling for 10,000 guineas at Tattersalls October Yearling Sale in 1982. *Chief Singer*, as the horse was duly named, turned out to be a top class racehorse, winning the Coventry Stakes at Royal Ascot as a two-year-old. The following year, he went on to become the second top-rated three-year-old in Europe, having accumulated over £250,000 in prize money and gained two Group 1 victories.

His credentials thus well established, *Chief Singer* was sold in the heady days of the bloodstock boom to stand as a stallion in Newmarket. Jeff Smith then purchased Littleton Stud in Hampshire, and a band of broodmares. The theory behind these purchases was that it is easier to breed a good winner than to pick out another yearling at the sales who would prove as successful as *Chief Singer*. Among the band of mares so shrewdly selected by Jeff Smith's advisers was *Peckitt's Well*, purchased for 24,000 guineas. That mare's mating with *Song*, then resident stallion at Littleton Stud, resulted in *Lochsong*. This filly was plagued with leg problems early in her career and, having wavered on the decision of whether to sell her, Jeff Smith kept her in training. Having won two small races as a three-year-old, she came up trumps at four, winning an unprecedented treble of the Stewards Cup, the Portland Handicap and the Ayr Gold Cup.

Lochsong then went from strength to strength. In 1993, as a five-year-old, she won two Group 1 races, a Group 3 and a Listed race, and was placed in a further five Group races. Christened 'The Queen of Speed' and voted the Cartier Horse of the Year, she started her six-year-old career in fine style, winning the Group 3 Palace House Stakes first time out, and following up with another three Group 1 wins. Her winning the Prix de l'Abbaye at Longchamp for the second year running was one of those highly emotional occasions that will remain in the hearts and minds of all racing enthusiasts. Although she failed in her attempt to win the Breeders Cup Sprint in America, she remains a champion by any standards. Now she is retired to stud, her offspring are eagerly awaited.

In the meantime, another of the original broodmare purchases, *Manx Millenium*, had produced an attractive chesnut filly, *Blue Siren*. She was entered for the Nunthorpe Stakes on the basis that she had every chance of coming second to *Lochsong*, thus collecting both first and second for her owner. With *Lochsong's* demise, *Blue Siren* burst through to win the race by a length and a half, only to be placed second after a stewards enquiry and objection found that her jockey had unfortunately barged his way between two horses to get a clear run to the line.

Added to this tally of winners is *Dashing Blade*, a triple Group 1 winner out of *Sharp Castan*, another of the original band of mares. *Dashing Blade* was champion two-year-old colt in Ireland in 1989 and won six races and £369,910 between the ages of two and four, over distances ranging from six furlongs to a mile and a half. Having stood his first season as a stallion at Littleton Stud, he is now at stud in Germany. *Sharp Castan*, in the meantime, has produced yet another Group winner, *Royal Solo*, a colt by top sire *Sadler's Wells*.

Yet another of the original mares, *On The Tiles*, produced a Group 1 winner in the filly *Air De Rien*. This filly did not race in Jeff Smith's colours, having been sold as a yearling, and she could well have been a deciding factor in the policy he has now adopted to race every horse be breeds before making a decision to sell. It remains to be seen whether *On The Tiles* will produce a Group winner to race in Jeff's colours, but that is the fascination of breeding. Added to the fascination is the expense: the cost of maintaining the broodmare band and the stud farm itself, and the training fees for the thirty-strong band of horses in training.

Another success story from an unlikely breeding source arose in 1993, when James Mursell's *Hard To Figure* won the Ayr Gold Cup, Europe's richest sprint handicap. *Hard To Figure* was bred to win three-mile steeplechases, but nobody told him that! His dam, *Count On Me*, won a lowly hurdle race at Newton Abbot, went lame in both forelegs and was sold to James Mursell by her trainer, Ron Hodges. *Hard To Figure*, whose full brother is a point-to-pointer, has won numerous races for his owner, who still breeds from *Count On Me* and her daughter, *Cedar Lady*.

What Jeff Smith and James Mursell have in common is a passion for the sport of racing. They are both unashamedly in love with it and both have chosen to perpetuate this love by breeding their own racehorses. They will freely admit that it costs them 'an arm and a leg' to indulge their passion but, win or lose, they are both determined to carry on with their investments for as long as it holds that allure – which probably means the rest of their lives.

Selling a foal or yearling well is hugely exciting and satisfying for the breeder. For the few minutes that a yearling is in the sales ring the atmosphere can become electric as the bidding goes higher and higher. Although breeders will have a fair idea of the market value of their wares, a horse is worth whatever someone wants to pay at the time of sale. All you need is two bidders with deep pockets who are equally intent on buying your horse.

I remember very well when David Gibson and Robert Percival offered a yearling colt by *Petong* at Tattersalls Houghton Sale. The colt was, admittedly, extremely good looking and expertly prepared by Robert, but the highest price for a *Petong* yearling up until then had been 30,000 guineas. Imagine their elation when the bidding went up to 50,000 . . . 80,000 . . . 100,000, with the hammer finally coming down at 125,000 guineas. A double delight for the breeders, who owned not only the mare but also *Petong* who, at that time, stood for a fee of £3,000.

Despite such success stories, however, most profits (if any) are more modest. Unless you invest heavily to begin with and aim to sell your produce at the Houghton Sales (where the 1995 average was 80,940 guineas), the average prices realised at the other yearling sales are a more realistic guide. In 1995, the average price for a yearling at the Doncaster St. Leger Sale was 8,810 guineas, and at the Newmarket October Sale, 16,965 guineas.

Sales proceeds and prize money for winning owner-breeders are not the only potential sources of income for the racehorse breeder. The British European Breeders' Fund, to which stallion owners contribute on an annual basis, offered breeders' prizes totalling £263,190 for two-year-old races alone in 1995. In addition, a number of race sponsors have increased their sponsorship to include a breeder's prize. In 1993, the Horserace Betting Levy Board introduced a prize money scheme for British breeders. The conditions of the scheme are still evolving, but currently embrace ' . . . The Levy Board's remit towards improvement in the quality of British-produced stock against the yardstick of racecourse performance'.

If, as a breeder, you are willing and financially able to keep one or more of your produce to race, you will enter a whole new realm of the breeding and racing world. When you have decided which trainer to use, they will advise you on how to proceed. Unless you have the knowledge and facilities to break in your own stock, your potential winner will go into training as a yearling or a two-year-old. As we are concentrating on flat racing (and unless you have set out specifically to breed a two-mile stayer), your charge is likely to be campaigned on the racecourse as a two-year-old. If you have set out to breed a precocious two-year-old, your trainer is likely to want the animal sooner rather than later. From the time your horse arrives at the training yard (and subject to the policy of your trainer), you will have the opportunity to visit the yard regularly to assess progress. If you want to see your horse work on the gallops, be prepared for early mornings; racing yard routine is pretty universal, and all the horses will be back from exercise by mid-morning.

If you are in the habit of having a 'flutter' at the races, you will now be in mortal danger from the temptation of betting on the basis of what you see on the gallops. Although a trainer relies on confidentiality, if you watch your horse work regularly with other animals you cannot help but get some idea of the ability of those other horses. There is nothing to stop you assessing these animals and taking your chance with the bookies, but remember – there is no such thing as a certainty!

With the start of the season looming, your trainer will talk you through the possible targets for your horse. Lengthy discussions are likely, concerning the distance to which your horse will be best suited, preferred ground conditions and which course is a likely starting place. You will quickly see how trainers earn their keep; the job is not as simple as some people believe! Beyond your legitimate areas of interest, remember that the trainer is the professional and, like the stud manager, should be left to get on with the job.

The first two-year-old races of the season are run over the minimum distance of five furlongs. The six- and seven-furlong races come only later in the season so, unless your trainer thinks your horse has sufficient speed for the five-furlong dash, be prepared to wait a while. You may also be forced to wait through setbacks in the form of injury, a cough and cold, or other viral problems. No matter how well they are looked after, these equine athletes can be afflicted by any or all of these problems, so patience is a real virtue among owners.

If all goes well, your horse will probably be entered in more than one race, the decision about which to opt for being made as late as one day before the event. As that day approaches, the excitement will build slowly but surely until, all at once, the day has arrived – you have your first runner!

Your trainer will have given you some idea of what to expect from your horse, based on work at home, but the competition in these two-year-old races is an unknown quantity. You can make certain assessments based on breeding and who trains each horse, but what you or the trainers won't know is how each animal will handle the added pressure of a real race meeting. Some two-year-olds take their first outing in their stride, travelling calmly in the horsebox, walking round the paddock like seasoned campaigners, cantering quietly to the start. Others, however thorough their background education, will become overexcited by the whole thing; the journey, the crowds around the parade ring and the public address system. Hopefully, your horse will have the temperament to cope with all these distractions in a relaxed and sensible manner, conserving his energies for the race to come.

As an owner, you will be able to join your trainer at the pre-parade ring, watch while your horse is saddled up, take your place in the centre of the parade ring and meet the jockey, who will receive his riding instructions from the trainer and discuss race tactics. He will, of course, be sporting your very own colours, which you have chosen and registered with Weatherbys.

This is it. Your first runner. Your first winner? The chances are that you will have an also-ran but there is always another race, another day. If you strike it lucky first time out, you will, no doubt, be hooked for life. If your horse manages a second or third place, or ran really well first time out, you will already be looking forward to the next time. For now, it is time to retire to the owners' and trainers' bar; to toast your success or drown your sorrows. Either way, it will be a magical day. Cost – what cost?

Before we get too carried away, it is as well to bring in a note of caution. For every race, there is only one winner and one first prize. Second and third place money can accumulate nicely if your horse is consistent, but it is more likely that your horse will lose more often than he wins. A loser costs as much to keep in training as a winner – and there are lots of losers.

Despite that note of gloom, there is no getting away from the fact that going racing as an owner is a totally different experience from going as a non-owner. It is, as the saying goes, the taking part that counts, not the winning! If you enter the game with the realistic view that it will cost you a lot of money with little, if any, return on your investment, then every winner, every good sale, will come as a wonderful bonus.

The racing industry is trying hard at present to make the sport more 'user-friendly' but, however hard they try, there is no substitute for being an active player. To go racing as Joe Bloggs is not a cheap day out. Getting there is relatively straightforward and, as a rule, the car parking is free; it is entry to the racecourse itself that you will pay for. If you don't have a car, buy a racing paper which will tell you how to get to the course of your choice by road, rail – or even air!

When you get to the turnstiles, you are offered the choice of a badge – which is not as self-explanatory as it sounds. 'Members' or 'Club' badges can, with very few exceptions, be purchased for the day by anyone, provided they are 'suitably' dressed (usual requirements are a jacket and tie or polo neck – no jeans, etc.). Depending on the individual racecourse, you will then have a choice of 'Grandstand and Paddock', 'Tattersalls', 'Silver Ring' or 'Course Enclosure'. There may also be a 'Family Enclosure' or 'Silver Ring and Park', or various parts of the course which are differently priced. Then there are courses that have their own names for the different grades of access. Goodwood, for instance, has a 'Richmond Enclosure', 'Gordon Enclosure' and 'Public Enclosure'. The Richmond Enclosure is for daily or annual members – except that only annual members are admitted during 'Glorious Goodwood' week in July.

To avoid disappointment or disillusionment – or being muscled away from certain areas by burly officials – a telephone call to the racecourse itself on the morning of racing should provide you with an explanation of what is on offer at what price. Access to the whole of the racecourse complex (except areas for owners, trainers, jockeys and officials) is generally gained through a Members or Club badge which, I believe, is worth paying the extra for if you want to make the most of your day.

However, if you are an owner-breeder, owner or, in some welcome cases, simply the breeder of a runner, you will be entitled to a number of complimentary badges (usually four for an owner and one for a breeder). Sporting your badge, you will have access to pretty much anywhere on the racecourse and can enjoy mingling not only with the crowd, but with other owners and trainers. You may receive an invitation from the sponsor of the race in which your horse is running; lunch, drinks, whatever – and they will look after you well. Sponsors will want to make the most of the facilities on offer at a racecourse. You could find yourself having a drink with celebrities from stage and screen or from the wider world of sport. If you are lucky enough to have a winner on a televised race day, you could find yourself staring at the camera and being interviewed by a BBC or Channel 4 commentator – so always remember to set up the video before leaving home!

On the subject of sponsors, racehorse owners are now allowed to sport a sponsor's logo on their colours, on the rugs or blankets worn by their horses in the paddock, and on the clothing worn by the horse's attendant. This really came about as part of the deal that allowed owners to register their racing activities for VAT, enabling them to claim back the VAT on all training and related costs. Of course it works both ways, and, strange though it sounds, VAT is now added to the prize money!

Finding a sponsor for a racehorse, or string of racehorses, is proving more difficult than you might at first imagine. Although there is plenty of televised racing, you would need to own a highly successful horse for the advertiser's logo to be seen often and close enough to be decipherable. And we all know there is no such thing as a racing certainty!

Should you find yourself with a very good horse, your trainer may suggest competing in a race abroad. The prize money on offer in the French and German Group races is worth the effort. You will, of course, have the considerable expense of transporting your horse to the racecourse and, if you want to cheer him home, the cost of getting there yourself. A trainer with a runner in Europe will usually make use of private aircraft hire, particularly if there is another British runner with whose connections such facilities can be shared. A six-seater light aircraft might, for example, take two trainers, two jockeys and two owners, so the individual cost will reduce appreciably. If the horses win or are placed, then the outing is tremendous fun and will probably have paid for itself. If they lose, it's another expense to put down to experience!

If, as a breeder, you keep and race fillies and one of them turns out to be really successful, you will be faced with the agonizing decision of whether to keep her and breed from her, or to sell her. The decision will generally be decided by the state of your finances, and even the 'big guns' need to balance their books. Robert Sangster, one of the biggest British breeders in the business, bred a filly named *Balanchine*, whom he sold privately to Sheikh Mohammed as a two-year-old. She went on to win the Oaks and the Irish Derby at three!

It is rare these days for high class racehorses to be sold at public auction. The best-bred fillies who become top class racehorses will almost inevitably be owned by people who can afford to retain them after racing, thereby enhancing their own broodmare bands. The best colts will, of course, be snapped up by the stallion buyers. When good fillies do become available on the open market, you can expect some fierce competition amongst bidders. At Tattersalls December Sales in 1992, some

If you find yourself with a very good horse, your trainer may suggest competing in a race abroad.

exceptional fillies were offered for sale. Among them was *Lyric Fantasy*. The same filly who was sold as a yearling at Doncaster for 12,500 guineas was sold to a partnership at the end of her two-year-old career for 340,000 guineas!

For every breeding success story there are hundred of failures. Mares fail to get in foal; accidents happen and horses are lost; foals and yearlings fail to make their reserve at the sales and potential racing stars fail to make their mark. The costs of keeping mares, buying stallion nominations, sales preparation and training fees go up rather than down. Why, then, do breeders keep going? There are ups and there are downs; there is good luck and bad luck; for every winner there are hundreds of losers. But for every breeder, a winner brings that unique sense of achievement, that spine-tingling thrill that proves it is possible. What chance of breeding and owning a *Lochsong*? A chance in a lifetime – but a chance, nonetheless.

USEFUL ADDRESSES

The British Horseracing Board,
42, Portman Square,
London, W1H 0EN.

The Federation of Bloodstock Agents (G.B.) Ltd.,
The Old Brewery,
Hampton Street,
Tetbury,
Glos. GL8 8PG.

The National Stud,
Newmarket,
Suffolk, CB8 0XE.

The Thoroughbred Breeders' Association,
Stanstead House,
The Avenue,
Newmarket,
Suffolk, CB8 9AA.

Weatherbys Group Ltd.,
Sanders Road,
Wellingborough,
Northants. NN8 4BX.